Elizabeth

Master Your Mindset

Thank you
for your leadership!

Molly

Master Your MINDSET

How Women Leaders Step Up

MOLLY GIMMEL

LIONCREST
PUBLISHING

MASTER YOUR MINDSET

How Women Leaders Step Up

FIRST EDITION

ISBN   978-1-5445-2899-1   *Hardcover*
        978-1-5445-2900-4   *Paperback*
        978-1-5445-2901-1   *Ebook*

This book is for the next generation of women leaders—you've got this!

CONTENTS

Introduction

WHAT MAKES A STRONG LEADER?

STEP INTO YOUR LEADERSHIP

"We need to reshape our own perception of how we view ourselves. We have to step up as women and take the lead."

—BEYONCÉ

Leadership is hard. Being a good leader is even harder.

People are relying on you. Your decisions shape the future of their lives, their careers, and their financial security. Your actions dictate how they feel about themselves, their abilities, and their future.

It's a heavy weight to carry. A weight that many people don't want to carry. A weight that many people don't carry well.

In June 2020, I finished six years of service as a member of the National Board of Directors of the National Association of Women Business Owners (NAWBO), including one year as chair of the Board. NAWBO represents women entrepreneurs, with over fifty chapters across the country that provide educational programming and networking for its members. On the national level, NAWBO advocates for legislation that helps small businesses, provides a wealth of educational resources for entrepreneurs, and offers a community of support to its members.

I've been a member of the organization since 2002. During this time, in addition to serving on the National Board, I've also served as president and as a member of my local chapter board, as a member of the Presidents Assembly Steering Committee (PASC) (NAWBO's peer support group for chapter presidents), and as chair of the PASC.

Also, since 2002, my business partner Diana Dibble and I grew our business from $350K to around $10M in annual revenue, making the Inc. 5000 list four years in a row. Our clients are leaders in US government agencies and the military. Prior to starting my company, I spent eight years working in the federal practices of three of the "Big Six" accounting/consulting firms. In my thirty-year career, I've seen and interacted with many different leaders in a lot of different settings.

As my term on the NAWBO Board was ending, I gave a lot of thought to the concept of leadership. How was it that a previously growing and thriving local chapter was struggling just a few years later? Or conversely, a local chapter that was struggling is growing and thriving a few years later? What makes one company grow quickly, and a similar one stagnate? What accounts for the difference? Almost always, it's leadership. That begs the question: what makes a strong leader?

Several studies in the last few years have shown that people don't quit jobs because they don't like the company or because they want more money or better benefits. Most people quit jobs because they don't like their boss. Imagine how much your company's retention rate would increase if the boss was a better leader.

When I was an undergraduate business major, I was told that leaders are the ones with the vision who decide where an organization is going, and managers are the ones who implement that vision.

I read a lot of business books, and John Maxwell, who writes about leadership, says that leadership is not about position, but about influence. He posits that anyone is a leader if they can influence others to follow them.

So which is correct? What is a leader? And what attributes do leaders, specifically women leaders, need to be successful in their roles?

I conducted a poll of NAWBO members in our Facebook group, asking what characteristic is most important for a strong leader to possess. I gave a range of mindset and skill options, including vision, decisiveness, inclusivity, organizational skills, and empathy. I also allowed people to write in answers if they felt something was more important that was not on the list, resulting in several additional characteristics, including emotional intelligence, courage, confidence, backbone, and the ability to execute—excellent suggestions all! The two options that tied for the most votes were integrity and communication skills. These two options got way more votes than any of the others.

With all of these differing opinions about what leadership is and what makes a good leader, it's no wonder that there are so few truly effective leaders. Because the thing that makes it hard is not possessing just one key quality or skill that makes a great leader, it's possessing all (or most) of them. Someone of the utmost integrity will not be a great leader if they can't communicate effectively. Someone with stellar communication skills will not be a strong leader if they don't have a vision that inspires people.

So, in a nutshell, to be a strong, effective leader, you need to have a vision for your organization, have a plan to achieve the vision, have confidence that you can achieve it and that you're the right person to lead the charge (while staying humble, of course), clearly communicate the vision to inspire others to want to help you achieve it, *and* be the type of person that others want to follow—one who demonstrates integrity, decisiveness, inclusivity, authenticity, and empathy. Easy, right? Not so much.

LEADERSHIP MINDSETS AND SKILLS

Why is leadership so hard? Because it's rare for someone to have all of the necessary mindsets and skills to be a strong and effective leader. For the purposes of this book, I define a "mindset" as a mental attitude that someone holds about themselves and a "skill" as having a high aptitude for a task or activity.

The good news is that these mindsets and skills are not hereditary—they are all learnable. So how do you figure out where you are and what you need to improve?

Author Jen Hatmaker said, "In the world of leadership, connection is everything." At its most basic, leadership is about connection. You must connect with the people you lead, and they must connect with you. But before you can connect with others, you have to connect with yourself. That's why I decided to focus this book on developing those leadership mindsets—the mental attitudes you need to develop in order to connect with yourself and others, making you a stronger leader. My next book will focus on how to hone essential leadership skills.

I created a list of leadership mindsets and then had conversations about those attributes with female leaders from all walks of life—the corporate world, politics, entertainment, nonprofits, entrepreneurs, and leadership coaches. In this book, these leaders share their perspectives and insights on what makes those qualities important for effective leadership and impart stories from their own leadership journeys. You can learn more about these women leaders in Appendix A.

LEADERSHIP AND GENDER

"NAWBO gets the leader it needs when it needs it." This is a common saying in the organization, which has had a lot of leaders over the last forty-five years—a different one every year, in fact. And those leaders have all been very different. Some had great visions about what the organization could accomplish, like when they were the force behind the passage of HR 5050, the Women's Business Ownership Act, in 1988. Some have had great wells of empathy, which was necessary as members struggled through recessions, pandemics, and other hard times. Still others were able to confidently make difficult—but important—decisions about how to address internal and external challenges to the organization.

All leaders are different, just like all people are different, and there's not just one way to be a good leader. It's been shown time and again that women approach leadership very differently than men. If you google "leadership effectiveness by gender," there are dozens of pages of results linking to studies and articles that overwhelmingly agree that women are more effective leaders than men. Women leaders are generally more collaborative and people-oriented, while male leaders are typically more autocratic and transactional. Of course, there are always exceptions—some women are autocratic, and plenty of men are collaborative, but these are common differences between leaders of these two genders.

A study published in the *Harvard Business Review*[1] in 2019 found that women leaders scored higher than men in seventeen of the nineteen leadership capabilities ranked. The only two areas that men scored higher on were "technical or professional expertise" and "develops strategic perspective," although the differential between men and women on those two capabilities was slight.

The COVID-19 pandemic has highlighted the difference between male and female political leaders. A recent *U.S. News & World Report* article states that:

> Countries with women who are head of state such as Denmark, Finland, Iceland, New Zealand, Germany and Slovakia have been internationally recognized for the effectiveness of their response to the pandemic. These women leaders were proactive in responding to the threat of the virus, implementing social distancing restrictions early, seeking expert advice to inform health strategies and unifying the country around a comprehensive response with transparent and compassionate communication.[2]

In fact, Jacinda Ardern, the prime minister of New Zealand, was named "The World's Greatest Leader" by *Fortune* in 2021 due to her effective handling of the pandemic.

In the twentieth century, an autocratic and transactional approach to leadership was the norm in the corporate world, politics, community organizations, and families. Baby boomers made up the vast majority of the population, and it was the only approach they had ever known. Today, the adult world is a mashup of multiple generations—there are still plenty of boomers, but more people are in Gen X (born 1965–1979), millennials (born 1980–1995), and Gen Z (born after 1995). And non-boomer generations don't respond to that traditional leadership style in the same way. They want leaders who inspire them but also care about them, who ask for their input, and who make them feel that they are contributing to a greater good.

Speaking at a private event a few years ago, former President Barack Obama said, "I'm absolutely confident that if every nation on Earth was run by women, you would see a significant improvement across the board on just about everything...living standards and outcomes."

Prince Georges County in Maryland elected Angela Alsobrooks as its first female county executive in 2018. Prince Georges County is a county of one million people just outside Washington, DC, and is known for being one of the most affluent Black communities in the US. When Alsobrooks became county executive, she appointed Black women to twenty-two high-level positions in the county, including superintendent of schools, director of community relations, director of economic development, fire chief, county state's attorney, director of communications, and chief administrative officer. When she hired these women, Alsobrooks told them that she did so not because they were women or because they were Black, but because they were the best.

Since taking the reins of the county government, Alsobrooks

has focused on investing in education, infrastructure, and police reform, as well as the county's response to the COVID pandemic. She and her team of Black women leaders have received high praise from other leaders within the state of Maryland and from the citizens of her county for their effective pandemic response and for their skillful management of county agencies, which had previously been mired in charges of corruption and favoritism.

How is leadership different for female versus male leaders? In my opinion, effective male leaders need to have strong leadership skills (aptitude for the tasks) but don't necessarily have to connect with the people that they are leading, and they don't have to be the type of person that others want to follow. Even if they're jerks, people will follow them if they have a vision, a plan, confidence, and communication skills. This book focuses primarily on helping women become better leaders through my lessons learned, along with the wisdom and experiences shared by the amazing women I interviewed.

Steve Jobs is a perfect example of a well-respected male leader who was also a jerk. He was well known for having temper tantrums, yelling and cursing at people, refusing to let them take time off, and generally treating his employees like dirt. But people put up with it because they thought he was a genius and believed in his vision. Unfortunately, or fortunately, depending on your point of view, a woman who behaved that way would not get the same benefit of the doubt.

It's just a fact of our society that women are judged differently than men. Think about how negatively Marissa Mayer was portrayed as the CEO of Yahoo! for her less-than-perfect people skills and lack of empathy for her workers. Olalah Njenga, CEO of YellowWood

Group, a strategic planning consulting firm in Raleigh, NC, is one of the amazing female leaders I interviewed for this book; she confirmed my suspicions of this fact. She shared a story about a client who is a female business owner. The woman called Olalah after hurling a chair at one of her employees. Olalah told her client, "I wish you had called me before you hurled the chair," because doing so cost her $140,000 to settle out of court. A very different outcome than when Jobs threw things at his employees.

In an interview with CNBC, Indra Nooyi, former CEO of PepsiCo, talked about meeting Jobs; he told her that she should throw temper tantrums—yell and throw things—to express displeasure and make it clear when she felt strongly about something. She followed up by saying that she hasn't gone so far as to throw anything, but she has become more forceful about expressing her displeasure by occasionally pounding the table and using a curse word now and then.

She says it's because tantrums just aren't part of her personality, but I think it's also because she knows that she would be judged harshly and publicly for doing so. I think if she had had a tantrum and threw something at an employee, it would have been all over the business press, the stock price would've tanked, and she would have been fired. These stories highlight the fact that women leaders are judged by different standards than men.

Several of my conversations with the women leaders I interviewed centered around the differences between male and female leadership styles. Not surprisingly, these female leaders own their leadership positions and are succeeding greatly.

Kristina Bouweiri, the CEO of Reston Limousine and Founder of

Sterling Women in Sterling, VA, is one of these women. She hopes that, at some point in the future, the world will acknowledge what many of us already believe to be true in our hearts: that women are better leaders than men. As she notes, since we already have a good start with so many big companies run by women—Lockheed Martin, General Dynamics, and many others—hopefully, in another twenty years, it won't be that unusual. She believes that women's traits not only make them more effective leaders but also make the employees working for them happier. In fact, she attributes doubling the size of her company directly to treating employees better:

> When I joined Reston Limo, my husband was running it, and his leadership style was completely different from mine. He was very autocratic, yelled at people, and would fire them on the spot if they did something wrong. When I took over, I couldn't act like that. I wanted my people to be happy, and treated them with respect. And the company doubled in size in just a few years.

Who would you rather work for? Kristina or her autocratic husband, who must have been sowing fear into the hearts of his employees? It's not surprising then that a stark contrast between male and female leadership at this company and others would directly correlate to a more successful business and happier, respected employees.

Darla Beggs, CEO of ABBA Staffing in Dallas, TX, agrees that it is important for women to be leaders but acknowledges the many challenges. One of them is age. She notes that while young women today were raised to stand up for themselves, women "of a certain age" were raised to be polite and not pushy or stand their ground too much. Another challenge Darla highlights is one that many (or all) women are all too familiar with: there is no male equivalent to the word bitch. As Darla puts it, when someone stands up for themselves, the man is seen as a leader and "very forthright," but the woman is a bitch.

Darla used to work for a woman who had a coffee cup that said, "I bitch therefore I am." She tells the tale:

> She carried it into meetings, and I thought then, *I don't know that I'd ever have the nerve to carry that.* Now, twenty years later, I would, but back then, I would not have done that. I think it's important that women my age, or any age, understand they can be anything they want. Not that I wasn't told that, but the doors were not open. Today, the doors are open for young women. They really can be anything they want and do anything they want, and it's up to them to figure out whether that is owning your own business, working for someone else, or being a stay-at-home mom.

Monica Levinson, a movie producer in Los Angeles, CA, agrees with Darla that women need to lead differently than men. She says women must do it with a smile:

> Leadership roles in the film business: the landscape has changed over the last few years, but it's been mostly men in those positions. Not only is it mostly men in all leadership positions and all groups, but it's men in all positions below me, like crew members. I needed to get the respect of the crew, the Teamsters, the grips, the electric crew, and the camera crew. I needed them to listen to me. As a woman, I had to do it with an incredible smile, being as sweet as I could be but also playing a little dumb.
>
> If I was asking the Teamsters to do something, I'd say, "Oh my gosh, I don't know how to do this" or "This is amazing how you do

that," and appeal to their egos. Some of the Teamsters I've worked with are incredibly educated and amazing people. It's just that they seem to respond better when you're appealing to their ego.

Like the other women leaders, Monica also had to learn how to adapt her approach. She continued to use the successful tactic of appealing to egos:

> People would come in with massive chips on their shoulders, and I could see it from a mile away. I would change my tune to, again, appeal to their ego and say, "I don't know how you're going to do this. This is really difficult, but you are my champion. I can't believe you're going to achieve this. And thank you. What can I do to help?"

Monica found that this approach helped differentiate her behavior from the times when she needed to be tough. Because it was a contrast to her sweetness and collaboration at other times, it became more effective when she did need to get tough, and men would respond to it better because they knew she was serious during those times. She didn't need to throw chairs, and undoubtedly her approach was much more successful for her than throwing a tantrum would have been.

She shares an example of how this sweet attitude worked for her when she was working on the movie *Zoolander*:

> I had no budget to do a certain unit, and the Teamsters in New York started calling me Madam Bowfinger because they would ask me at the end of each day, "What do you need to for tomorrow?" And I'd say, "Nothing, I'm going to be good. I don't need anything for tomorrow." And then the next day, I'd say, "I just need that little stake bed. I'm just going to put a couple pieces of equipment on it.

I'm going to borrow one grip from your crew, is that okay? Thank you so much." And I would just do it very innocently and sweetly. That was how I had to get away with it.

Now, Monica has adapted her style slightly. She regrets some of the playing dumb and having to lead by taking a backseat, even to her bosses. Nonetheless, she still leads with a smile. And she is still tough when she has to be, but she starts with a smile. She is authentic (something we will discuss in further detail in Chapter 11) and makes sure she knows who everybody is. She doesn't stroke people's egos if she doesn't mean it anymore, but she is also the first one to tell people that they're doing a great job if they are. She knows it's really important people know she's on their side because it's not easy work and everyone is away from their families, on the road or out of town, and working very hard and very long hours. Unfortunately, some things haven't changed because, as Monica says, "a lot of men still don't take women seriously."

Like many women, Monica has also had to find ways to work around the obstacles placed in front of her. When she was working in comedy (again, with mostly men), she would try to give notes as she sat at the monitors during or post-production. She whole-heartedly feels that if she were a man, they would have openly accepted her earlier as part of their creative team. But they were unwilling to listen to her, so instead of giving notes directly to the director, she would pass them through someone else, even though her female perspective was very helpful when she was the only woman in a room full of men.

Monica shares another story to illustrate her point. Although it happened in the past, it could just as easily have happened yesterday to any number of women:

I was in a marketing meeting for a comedy movie that I was co-producing. My producing partner was a man, a lovely man and totally on my side and supported me my whole career, but he was getting up there in age, and I was in my forties, and we're in a marketing meeting with about eight men from the studio plus our director, who was probably about five or six years younger than me.

I had been through the process from the beginning with everybody, and I did not like the marketing campaign. I didn't like it. I thought that it was not going to appeal to our audience. And I had spent time speaking to twenty-five-year-olds to see about their recognition of the actors in the movie and whether something more subversive would work in terms of getting an audience in to see the movie. Anyway, I raised my hand in the meeting and said, "I have been speaking to people, and I don't think this campaign is the best we can do. I do think a more subversive image would be of interest." And I got cut off by the director, who said, "Who have you been speaking to, your Oprah's book club?" squarely putting me into old-woman territory. Him saying that gave the entire marketing team permission to laugh along with him. And also the permission to ignore everything else I said.

And this is a guy who I played poker with. He knew that I wasn't out of touch, but he didn't want to hear what I had to say. And he wanted to appear cool with his buddies at the studio. And by the way, the movie did not do well. The poster did not do well. And every time I wear the subversive image that they did on the T-shirt, people stop me on the streets.

Certainly, no one can put a numerical value to all the times when a woman's contributions have been overlooked but would have otherwise improved a course of action, but it must be very, very high.

A while back, Monica was a guest lecturer at a class at USC for a female professor who used to be a big producer in town. The professor asked, "What's it like being a woman in the industry?" Monica told that story as an example. The professor said, "Well, didn't you yell at them, and didn't you go back at them and call them out?" And Monica said, "No. Why? What would be the point? I just needed to keep going." The professor responded, "Well, that's why you're still working in the industry. And I'm not."

Monica explains her reaction this way:

> I thought that was really telling. I've been in this business so long, and I've worked with men for so long that I knew what they needed from me. They needed me to be resilient. They needed me to keep going. They needed me to not call them out on gender politics and just work hard. And yes, I did work harder than most of the men in the room. But not harder than the director, not harder than the other producers I was working with. I mean, certainly, I was earning my keep, but you know, I usually put up with it because I was working with people that were incredibly smart and talented, and I was choosing to let it go in an effort to work with the people that I thought were worth it.

In all likelihood, you've probably found yourself in similar situations to Monica, Kristina, or Darla. How did you handle it at the time? What would you have done differently knowing what you know now? What did the voice inside your head tell you at that time? In Chapter 1, we'll discuss mastering that mental chatter.

WHAT WILL YOU LEARN IN THIS BOOK?

Leadership is not just for those who are CEOs or political officials.

Leadership is needed at all levels in all areas of our society—in the government, the workforce, our schools, our communities, and our homes. Leadership is not just about a title or a position—anyone and everyone can be a leader in some way. Even if you don't have a leadership title at your job, you can offer to lead a project or suggest better ways to do things. Even if you don't have a job, you can take on leadership roles by volunteering for a local charity, starting a book club in your community, or organizing the talent show at your kids' school. If you have kids, by definition, you are a leader in your family, and you are setting an example for them every day.

Part 1 of this book, Chapters 1–8, is about connecting with yourself, which means seeing yourself as a leader. It starts by getting control of the voice in your head, then overcoming imposter syndrome, living with integrity, gaining confidence, learning how to be decisive, cultivating resilience, opening up to lifelong learning and growth, and figuring out how not to take things personally.

Part 2 of this book, Chapters 9–13, is about developing a mindset of connection with others, specifically with those we lead. The crux of connection with others is servant leadership, which means understanding that leadership is not about the leader—it is about serving the organization and people you lead. You connect and serve by demonstrating empathy, authenticity, approachability, and humility.

While leaders are often put on a pedestal, either by virtue of their title or because of their accomplishments, the fact is that all leaders are human beings with all the imperfections and flaws that come with being a person. Embracing your imperfections can help you understand yourself better and more strongly connect with the people you lead, both of which will make you a better leader. I hope this book helps you do just that.

I give you several takeaways in this book to help you improve as a leader. Finally, I provide a self-assessment you can use when you've completed the book to help you get started on where to direct your focus so you can begin improving your leadership mindset immediately.

A couple of caveats. First, I am not a scientist, a researcher, or a professor. The information in this book is not based on any studies that I conducted. I based it on my own experiences as a business and community leader; the lessons I've learned during my leadership journey; the books I've read, often written by the aforementioned scientists, researchers, and professors; and the insights and experiences shared with me by the leaders I interviewed while writing this book. Academic studies have their place, to be sure, but cold numbers don't always convey the human aspects of the relational parts of business. This book focuses mostly on the latter. Second, I haven't mastered all of these attributes myself. I'm better at some than others, while there are a few I really struggle with. Nobody is great at everything, and that's okay. The point is to identify those areas you need to improve in and make an effort to do so.

In the next book in this series, planned for publication in 2024, I will focus on the skills required for effective leadership—such as communication, negotiation, having difficult conversations, team building, and growing other leaders—and share the conversations I had with these same women leaders (and a few more) about the importance of mastering those skills in order to be a more effective leader.

You are already a leader. Now let's get started making sure you're the best leader you can be.

PART 1

CONNECTING WITH YOURSELF

Chapter 1

MASTER YOUR MENTAL CHATTER

HOW TO GET THE VOICE IN YOUR
HEAD TO BE ON YOUR SIDE

"Everyone has that inner voice, the one that's a Negative Nancy. I'd say to ignore that voice and to be confident and follow your heart."

—KATHARINE MCPHEE

Last weekend, I offered to help a friend with something, and she turned me down. But the way she declined seemed weird to me. So the next day, when I was thinking about it, I had a follow-up conversation with her. I asked her why she refused when the help I offered was something she needed, and she responded that she did need the help, just didn't want it from me. Then she accused me of having an underhanded ulterior motive for providing the help, and then she said some even nastier things, leaving me very upset and wondering if I should end our friendship completely.

The crazy thing is that this follow-up conversation took place entirely in my head. In reality, it never happened. Most likely, she declined my help because she no longer needed it, she seemed weird because she was thinking about something else, and she had no animosity toward me whatsoever. I had been bullied by my own brain.

Turns out that most of us have a voice in our head that talks to us nonstop—all day, every day. This is sometimes called our "inner voice" or our "inner critic" because the voice is often saying critical things about us. The term "mental chatter" refers to the fact that the voice is chattering away inside our heads all the time. In her book *The High 5 Habit*, Mel Robbins delves into the science behind the voice in our heads and why it is always talking to us.

Robbins also recommends that you give yourself a high five in the mirror every day. This repeated action slowly shifts your mind from only noticing your flaws when you look in the mirror to looking forward to seeing yourself and rooting for *you*. If you're interested in a deep dive into the science, this is a great resource.

Your thoughts are incredibly powerful. When you ponder the way your brain and our mental chatter can direct us—either positively or negatively—you can then understand why mastering your mental chatter is important to develop into a more effective leader.

I was introduced to the concept of mental chatter in a workshop called "Creativity & Personal Mastery," or CPM, taught by Dr. Srikumar Rao, author of *Are You Ready to Succeed?* In the workshop, we were given an exercise to do over a few weeks: set the alarm on your phone to go off several times a day at random times, and when it does, write down what the voice in your head is talking about.

I discovered that I was often having conversations in my head—sometimes replaying conversations I had previously had with others, other times imagining conversations that could maybe someday—but probably would not ever—take place. I also learned that I was regularly singing to myself, usually the same song, over and over. Talk about earworms!

One of the other people taking the workshop was a man who learned that every morning, while he was getting ready for his day, the voice was telling him how much he didn't want to go to work. He liked his job, he liked his coworkers, but after hearing the voice in his head tell him over and over and over that he didn't want to go to work, he had started to dread going to the office. Once he realized that the voice was sabotaging his career, he consciously decided to change it. He wrote, "I can't wait to go to work" on a sticky note, put it on his mirror, and repeated it over and over as he was getting dressed every morning. He quickly noticed a shift in his attitude in the morning and started looking forward to going to work.

Many people believe that if the voice in their head says something, it must be true. We've been told to trust our intuition, so if that's what the voice is saying, we should trust it, right? Luckily, that is not necessarily the case.

Elizabeth Bennett-Parker, the Vice Mayor of Alexandria, VA, told me that she has been fighting with her inner voice for a long time. She said,

> I am my own worst critic. I will beat myself up for things that I can rationally tell myself that no one else is thinking about this anymore or no one else even noticed that you said this word instead of that word. I assure myself they are not thinking about it, I need to move on, but I find it difficult to do so.

I think serving in public office in some ways has heightened that because I'm saying things in a much more public setting where more people are paying attention since our council meetings are videotaped. I don't think that many people actually watch them. But what I say lives on in a way that it did not before.

The fact is that your inner voice is usually repeating what it has heard from others in the past. So if you grew up with very critical parents who told you that you weren't smart or athletic, the voice heard that and continues to repeat it, even years later. If an ex-boyfriend or bully in school told you that you were ugly or stupid, the voice heard that, too, and repeats it. If you had a teacher who told you that you would never amount to anything or that your writing sucks, the voice remembers that and continues to repeat it. Our culture tells you that you have to be stick-thin and look like a supermodel to have value, and if you're chubby with average looks, the voice tells you that you're not good enough.

Bennett-Parker thinks that women are more self-critical than men,

> Because men don't really care what they look like. And I think that's a big one for women. I'm always like, "Oh, my hair looks horrible today. I've got bags under my eyes. This shirt is ugly." Whatever it might be. It's just constant. And all that extra energy that it takes.

She continues,

> For example, I recently went to an event, the Torpedo Factory's forty-fifth anniversary celebration. And the mayor couldn't be there because there were three other events happening that night. So I was there representing the City, and the invitation said, "Dress

to impress," and then it said most people will be in business attire. So I'd been running around that day—we'd had a city council meeting earlier—so I just stayed in what I was wearing, which was a dress and a blazer, and I had leggings and boots on. Then I got there, and I immediately felt underdressed because people were dressed much nicer. So the voice in my head was like, *Oh my God, I'm underdressed.* And I realized that I had heels in my car. So I went out and took off my leggings and boots and put on heels, and I immediately felt so much better. But the mental energy that I spent on that was crazy.

Even very successful people struggle to master their mental chatter. In several interviews, the singer Lizzo has talked about her battle with her inner voice. She said,

> I would watch things on television, and I would look at magazines, and I would not see myself. When you don't see yourself, you start to think something's wrong with you. Then you want to look like those things, and when you realize it's a physical impossibility, you start to think, *What the fuck is wrong with me?* I think that took a greater toll on me, psychologically, growing up than what anyone could have said to me.[3]

The Cambridge Dictionary defines "brainwashing" as "the process of making someone believe something by repeatedly telling them that it is true and preventing any other information from reaching them." Your own brain is brainwashing you by continually telling you negative things about yourself and blocking out anything you hear to the contrary.

No matter what that voice has heard in the past and is currently repeating back to you, however, *only you* can ultimately control what it says. This is why it is crucial to connect with yourself. Get in touch with that voice and make it work for you and not against you.

Dr. El Brown, Founder of KinderJam and host of the podcast, *Straight Talk with Dr. El*, in Fairfax, VA, had a lot of thoughts about how she manages her mental chatter. She recognized the importance of controlling the voice in her head at a very early age and now teaches her son, who is on the autism spectrum, how to do the same. Here's what she had to say:

> I think what most people have real trouble with is that the voice in their head is telling them negative things about themselves. You get that voice to stop doing that and just start saying positive things to start to make yourself believe in yourself and tell yourself that you believe in yourself.

> That's my gift. I believe in the power of words. I say the same thing to my son; your inner voice is the voice you hear the most. So you need to amplify it to say positive things about you. And I'm always honest with myself. It's because of my self-talk that I am the way I am because I had to become very honest about what I wanted in the world.

> When I was young, I grew up in an environment where there wasn't a lot of positive speak, and it wasn't necessarily directed to me; it was just the nature of oppression. People are used to saying things carelessly because things were said carelessly to them. As a young child, I was very precocious and labeled talented and gifted, but that was meaningless in my community. It just meant that I saw and thought differently.

> There were things that were said by people in my family. When I

was a child—six or seven years old—if I couldn't do something an adult had asked me to do, they would say, "You're not worth a plug nickel. You're not worth the food you eat." It was one of those colloquialisms that people said all the time, but I've always thought that words had meaning. Even at six and seven years old, I thought, one, that's not true, and two, I don't think you should say that to people. Even though the people around me said these derogatory things to each other all the time, it just never sat well with me.

When I got to be about eighteen years old, I made a decision to go to college, and I was a first-generation college student. In going to college, I knew that it was something that I would have to talk myself through. My parents, grandparents, and the rest of my family didn't know that I was going to college until a couple of weeks before I left, and I told them, "I'm going to college."

My grandmother's response was, "You ain't going to no damn college." But when she said it, it wasn't like she was saying, "I don't believe in you." I could have said, "Mimi, I'm going to the moon," because college was just as plausible and completely outside her scope of understanding. They had no frame of reference. They were like, "Who goes to college? Why would you go to college? How do you get to college? What does one do in college? That's people on TV." It was so abstract to her. And oddly enough, this same woman, if I were to tell her I was going to the moon today, she would be like, "She's gone to the moon."

I think that success is always relative to the individual's lived experience. So when I became a teacher, that was huge to her because for thirty years, she worked in a school's cafeteria. The teachers in her school, they were dressed really nice, and they had professional jobs. Then for me to become a classroom teacher in Japan, that was also huge. I think anything after that, each later accomplishment, was just another thing. But my being a teacher was so huge to her because there weren't very many African American teachers. She spent thirty years in the school's cafeteria, and now her granddaughter was one of the teachers. I wasn't a janitor; I wasn't a secretary; I wasn't an aide; I didn't work in the cafeteria. I was a teacher. Now, as Dr. El, she sees me as a teacher who teaches teachers, a teacher who teaches principals. So I think people's experiences of success are relevant to what they actualize based on their lived experience.

So because of that, I always have dialogues with myself. Very early on, I had to learn how to amplify my voice so that it was louder than the other voices of doubt. In turn, it was louder than any voice of doubt that I have because one of the things I've learned from experience is that my voice of doubt is seldom about me; it's a narrative that others have given me that resides in my head.

That's why I'm very deliberate and intentional about teaching teachers and parents how to speak to children because children are born a blank slate. All those words that you input into a child's brain become their inner thoughts, and in time, those inner thoughts can either move in a trajectory toward positive outcomes or can move a child's trajectory toward negative outcomes. It's really more complex than what I choose to say to myself. Anything that was told to me as a child may be potentially detrimental to my success.

My son is on the autism spectrum, and he has a belief in himself that is amazing to watch. But his belief in himself, whether he realizes it or not, is my belief in him manifested. He's now a teenager, and his belief in himself and his actions are because I've been his affirmative voice since before he was born. So he knows no other way of thinking about himself because he has a mother who thinks he's capable of anything that he wants to do. Even at three, I gave him a mantra: "I can be anything I want to be if I plan and work hard." I've been his buffer against anything that might tell him contrary.

That said, if you don't have that buffer based on the experiences that you had as a child, like I didn't, there is some intentionality that comes in developing that positive self-talk.

So I listen when my mind talks to me, and I organize when my mind talks to me, and I make sure that the loudest voice is my own. There's no voice louder than my own. My voice is always kind to me. I'm always kind to myself, and my voice has never, ever gotten me wrong. If I've ever made a mistake, it has always been because I have listened to an external voice, but my internal voice has never steered me wrong. Even if my voice is contrary to what social norms are, I listen to my voice. My internal voice is the most important voice to me.

Dr. Brown has learned how to get the voice in her head to support her instead of sabotage her. How can you do the same?

First, be aware of what your voice is saying and understand that you don't have to believe it. Try the exercise I talked about above to identify what your voice is regularly talking to you about.

Next, notice when the voice starts saying negative things and tell it to shut up. One way to do this is to name the voice. Calling it a different name reinforces that it's not omniscient—it's just a voice.

You could name it after someone you don't like or just pick a name at random, like Stan. Then, when it starts telling you that you're fat or stupid, talk back to it and say, "Screw you, Stan, I look great" or "Screw you, Stan, I'm doing a great job."

By thinking of the voice as Stan, you can start reacting to it differently. Would you talk to one of your friends or family members the way Stan talks to you? I hope not! And I hope you wouldn't let someone else talk to you that way either. If not, then why do you accept it from Stan?

Re-brainwash Stan into thinking you're the greatest thing since sliced bread by using positive messages instead of negative. Create affirmations and repeat them constantly. Put them on your phone wallpaper or your computer screensaver, or write them on sticky notes and put them all over your home and office. Affirmations don't have to be complicated; they can be as simple as, "I am smart, I am strong, I can handle whatever comes my way."

It won't happen overnight, but consistent effort will transform Stan into your biggest fan, which will help you be a more effective leader.

CHAPTER TAKEAWAYS

→ Most people believe that if the voice in their head says something, it must be true. They especially believe it when the voice tells them negative things about themselves. This can lead to a lack of self-esteem, a lack of confidence, and it can cause or exacerbate anxiety and depression.

→ The voice in your head often repeats what it has heard other people say. That doesn't make it correct.

→ Name the voice so you can reply to it as if to another person. If you wouldn't let someone else talk to you like Stan does, don't let Stan talk to you that way.

→ Create affirmations and repeat them constantly to brainwash Stan into supporting you instead of sabotaging you.

→ Try Mel Robbins' recommendation and give yourself a daily high five in the mirror.

Chapter 2

OVERCOME IMPOSTER SYNDROME

YOU ARE NOT A FRAUD

"I have varying degrees of confidence and self-loathing. I often doubt my talent…and fear they're going to find out that I don't know what I'm doing."

—MERYL STREEP

When I was an undergrad at the College of William & Mary, I wasn't a great student. Not at the bottom of my class, but definitely not at the top either; I was right in the middle. In high school, I hadn't had to work very hard to get good grades, and I preferred spending my time in the theater and with my friends over studying or doing homework. So when I got to college, I wasn't prepared for how rigorous it would be academically, and I still preferred hanging out with my friends to studying. So when senior year came along, and the big consulting firms and multinational corporations came to do on-campus interviews, I signed up for a bunch of them and didn't get a single follow-up call. They were only interested in the students in the top 20 percent of the class.

I graduated into the middle of a recession, and jobs weren't plentiful, so I moved back home and went back to the company I had worked at for the previous four summers, doing title searches at the county courthouse. After a while, I managed to get a job working for a small company that supported the Defense Department (I live in the Washington, DC, area, so a large percentage of the population is either government employees or government contractors). While there, I managed to impress the chief operating officer (COO) with how quickly I learned the federal regulations governing what we did and with the quality of my work. After I had been there about eighteen months, the COO left the company and told me that when I was ready to leave, I should get in touch with him, and he would bring me on board at his new company.

I was ready to leave then, but I didn't say anything because he was going to KPMG. KPMG was one of those firms that had interviewed me on campus and hadn't wanted me, so Stan was telling me not to bother calling. It took me six months to talk myself into calling him, but I eventually did, and KPMG hired me. For a while after I started, I felt like a fraud. I didn't believe that I really belonged there or that I was as smart and as good at my job as the people who had been hired on campus, but eventually, I did believe it.

Two years later, when Arthur Andersen called to recruit me away from KPMG, even though Andersen hadn't wanted me in college either, I jumped at the opportunity and ended up spending five really valuable years there. My experiences at Andersen gave me the confidence to walk into almost any room and not feel like an imposter. I own that I'm not great at everything, and I'm okay with that. I don't have to pretend like I am perfect to be respected for what I do bring to the table.

Imposter syndrome is the feeling that you are not qualified to be in the position you're in, that you're sure that people will figure out that you're a fraud or an imposter. It often occurs when someone is put into a leadership position for the first time or into a new role that they don't feel ready for.

Imposter syndrome was first defined in 1978 in the article "The Impostor Phenomenon in High Achieving Women: Dynamics and Therapeutic Intervention" by Dr. Pauline R. Clance and Dr. Suzanne A. Imes, and it was originally thought to be something suffered exclusively by women.[4] Further research over the years has concluded that men suffer from it as well. In fact, up to 70 percent of all people have it at some point in their lives.[5]

Even super successful people can have imposter syndrome. Many famous people have talked about it in speeches and interviews. Even Supreme Court Justice Sonia Sotomayor talks about having "a touch" of imposter syndrome when she was going through the Senate confirmation process.

In an interview with the online magazine *Rookie* in 2013, Emma Watson said,

> It's almost like the better I do, the more my feeling of inadequacy actually increases, because I'm just going, any moment, someone's going to find out I'm a total fraud, and that I don't deserve any of what I've achieved. I can't possibly live up to what everyone thinks I am and what everyone's expectations of me are. It's weird—sometimes [success] can be incredibly validating, but sometimes it can be incredibly unnerving and throw your balance off a bit, because you're trying to reconcile how you feel about yourself with how the rest of the world perceives you.[6]

Lena Dunham told *Glamour* magazine in 2017:

> Making my deal with HBO as a twenty-three-year-old woman, I
> felt that I had so much to prove. I felt like I had to be the person
> who answered emails the fastest, stayed up the latest, worked the
> hardest. As much as I loved my job, I really, like, injured myself in
> some ways. If I had felt like, "You're worthy of eight hours of sleep,
> not four; you're worthy of turning your phone off on a Saturday," I
> don't think it would have changed the outcome of the show. [But]
> I could have worked with a sense of joy and excitement, rather
> than guilt and anxiety of being "found out." The advice I would
> give any woman going into a job if she has a sense of impostor
> syndrome would be: "There will be nothing if you don't look out
> for you." And I can't wait, on my next project, to go into it with
> the strength that comes from valuing your own body and your
> own mental health.[7]

Successfully confronting and defeating imposter syndrome is
another way in which we must connect with ourselves to be effective leaders. Seek to look inside yourself to discover why you feel
like an imposter. Ask yourself questions about why you feel the
way you do. Do you think it was just a lucky break (or breaks) that
landed you where you are today? From an outside perspective, I
can tell you that is unlikely. It's almost certain you didn't get where
you are by sheer luck alone either.

Lauren Weiner, CEO of WWC Global, a Defense contracting firm
in Tampa, FL, told me a story about her experience with imposter
syndrome. She said,

> When I was in my PhD program at Dartmouth, the woman who
> coined the phrase "imposter syndrome" and did all of the major

research on it came to do a brown bag workshop. I was sitting at the table, hoping nobody would look at me or they'd figure out *I* was actually the imposter. I very clearly missed the concept of the talk because I was so terrified of being found out. Is that irony?

I asked her why she felt like an imposter, and she responded,

Because I didn't think I deserved to be in that program, in that room, at that table. Even though I had succeeded at every point in my life to that juncture, I thought it was somehow that I had lucked into it, that people were just being nice, that everyone else had "it," and I was just faking my way along.

I knew objectively I belonged, but there was (at that point particularly) some thought that somehow I had just tricked everyone into thinking I belonged. I definitely felt that way early in my career as well. I was objectively extremely successful and fit into my cohort well, but they all seemed to have it together. By outward appearances, so did I, and I didn't realize that I was only seeing their outward appearance as well. I think it took some honest talks with peers to see that they had the same doubts that I did. That nobody was as together in their mind as they appeared and that was actually success. If we knew how to handle everything, we weren't growing and maturing, but that growth was messy.

I asked her if she still felt like an imposter, and she answered,

No, I've lost almost all of that over the last twenty years, and I generally own where I am and how I've gotten there...but every once in a while, I do have a moment of "How the heck did I get here, and why does everyone seem to think I know what I'm doing?!" I talk a lot about that to other young women. There's a whole lot of "faking it until you make it" that happens legitimately in successful people. You can't know every answer to every sticky question.

As Lauren mentions, one way people recommend getting over imposter syndrome is to fake it till you make it. Pretend like you believe you belong, and you're just as qualified as everyone else, and eventually, you'll start to actually believe it. As we discussed in the previous chapter, your inner voice is very powerful, and if you tell yourself something enough times, you'll eventually believe it. If you're not comfortable with that, just give it time. Imposter syndrome generally fades as you gain more experience and self-confidence from seeing that you do actually have what it takes to get the job done and done well.

At an event in London during her book tour in 2018, Michelle Obama talked about how she got past imposter syndrome when she became First Lady and was dealing with very accomplished people:

> I have been at probably every powerful table that you can think of, I have worked at nonprofits, I have been at foundations, I have worked in corporations, served on corporate boards, I have been at G-summits, I have sat in at the UN. Here's the secret: they're not that smart. There are a lot of things that folks are doing to keep their seats because they don't want to give up power. And what better way to do that than to make you feel you don't belong…you have to prepare yourself, because when you get those arrows thrown at you, all you can fall back on is your experience and your ability.

Lisa Marie Platske, a leadership coach and the President of Upside Thinking, a leadership consultancy in Alexandria, VA, told me that she really suffered from imposter syndrome when starting her business because her business was very different from her previous career in federal law enforcement, and she didn't think she had the right credentials to be credible. Without a business degree or even any business experience, she worried that she wouldn't make enough money to support herself:

> Imposter syndrome was really strong. I constantly told myself, *You're not good enough, you're not smart enough, you'll never figure this out.* I felt like this because I didn't have the pedigree. I didn't have the connections.

> When I put on my first event, I gave away so many tickets because I wanted to be generous. At the end of the event, I had a ten-thousand-dollar bill, and I had to take out a business loan. It just didn't even dawn on me that there'd be the consequence at the end from wanting to be generous—because I didn't understand business from a tangible standpoint. Then I felt crappy about myself, thinking that if only people knew how little I knew about what I was doing.

> For a good year and a half or longer, my conversations with my husband, Jim, at the dinner table were up and down. "This is the greatest thing. This is awful. I'm a failure. This is the greatest thing. I don't have any clue what I'm doing."

> One day, after a few years, he said, "I'm done. I'm tired of this conversation. You're either in or you're out. You're either doing the business or you're not doing the business, but I'm not having this conversation every time that you're not feeling it, telling you how great and capable and wonderful and able you are."

> The conversation with Jim was truly the "Come to Jesus" moment. I can't say it stopped then. What it did was it put me at the edge of

the cliff—are you in or are you out? Are you really committed to doing this or are you really committed to your sad story? I decided that I can really make a difference. I can do this. There still were a lot of bumps and a lot of bruises and a lot of failures. But it was that moment in time where I decided I was in, and I can do it, and I stopped thinking of myself as an imposter.

Jenni Romanek, the Director of Analytics for Instagram, told me that she discovered early in her career that just about everybody has imposter syndrome. Which meant to her that if everybody feels like they're an imposter, that can't possibly be true because there's no chance that every single living human is an imposter. Before joining Instagram, she worked at Facebook and told me this story:

> When I started at Facebook, one of the reasons I took the job is that I was really inspired by this woman named Cheryl, who was director of analytics for the Facebook ads team who had interviewed me. We really hit it off, and when I was deciding whether or not to make the move from Twitter, she did a phone call with me. It was on a Sunday afternoon, and I later learned that she had had a couple of glasses of wine sitting in her backyard.
>
> And we had this really brutally honest conversation where she told me about the times when she had left meetings crying, how she had felt really alone because her peer set was, at the time, all men. And I was just totally enamored of her, and I was like, "Oh my gosh, this woman's badass. She's doing such a cool job, and she's being really open about the challenges but also telling me she really loves her job." So she became a really good friend and mentor from that moment on. And I decided to roll. And I remember a couple months into working with her at some point over tea, she shared with me how much she felt like an imposter.

It shook me to my core because she was beloved. She had a team of three hundred people. I can't imagine a leader who people liked working with more. And I just felt like, "No, you're not an imposter. You're so real, and that's what people really like about you." And it was just the light bulb of, *Wow, Cheryl feels this way.*

I also remember having that conversation with a male colleague who was a director of engineering who people were kind of scared of, who came off sounding very confident. He didn't speak up much in meetings, but if he spoke up, he had something really smart to share. As we got to be friends, at some point, he shared with me that he felt this immense sense of imposter syndrome. And it was shocking to me because it was so diametrically opposed to how everybody viewed him.

I also had this idea in my mind at the time that if you are a successful, wealthy, confident-sounding, straight, white male, then there's no way in hell that you had imposter syndrome. But it's so prevalent that we all share it but are too embarrassed to talk about it. That was just another light bulb moment of knowing that this is something everyone deals with, which means that we're actually all good enough. And we're all kind of getting in our own way. Figuring that out helped me get over it.

Jenni's point about discovering that almost everyone has imposter syndrome was interesting to me because, in my interviews for this book, I was shocked at how many of the women leaders I spoke to admitted that they had suffered from it during their careers. Probably the most surprising to me was when I spoke to Melanie Thomas Armstrong, who had been the youngest woman ever to make partner at Arthur Andersen in the practice I worked in. I had always seen her as being supremely competent and confident, and to find out that she felt imposter syndrome was not something I was expecting when we talked. She told me:

> When I made partner at Andersen in 2001, I had really wanted to make partner, and I made partner. But the whole time, I actually felt like I didn't deserve to have made partner. I had the feeling I wasn't good enough to make partner and somehow scammed my way into making partner. Then, of course, the firm went under with the Enron thing, and the practice was acquired by Unisys. And then, I went to PwC, and they offered me the position of a managing director (MD) [which is a lower level than a partner]. I was happy and took the job. I would never have pushed them to bring me on as a partner. I didn't feel like I should be. Then I decided that I wanted to be a partner again. And then when I made partner again, I went, *Oh my God, maybe I wasn't a fraud because I made partner twice.* Then I thought about it and realized I was just as accomplished as the other people who made partner.

> When I made partner for the second time, I realized it wasn't a fluke. I went to PwC as an MD, and it took me three years to make partner there. Two men came in right after I did, also as MDs from other firms, and six months later, they were announced as new partners. They negotiated it as part of their employment agreement. Basically, if they didn't set the building on fire for six months, they were going to be named partners. That would never have occurred to me. And I think that was a big shock for me. I would never negotiate myself into a partnership. Because then I would have felt more like an imposter. I had to earn it and know that I had earned it. I couldn't feel good about it if I hadn't done that.

Recently, researchers have started to push back on the concept of imposter syndrome as a problematic notion, some saying that it's actually a good thing and others saying it's an invented concept created to make women feel less confident about themselves.

In his book *Think Again*, Wharton professor Adam Grant states that having imposter syndrome can be beneficial, especially for people early in their careers, because it causes them to be more careful and thorough in their work. He cites a study showing that medical residents with imposter syndrome make fewer mistakes and have a better bedside manner with patients than residents who are more confident in their abilities.

In 2021, the *Harvard Business Review* published an article called "Stop Telling Women They Have Imposter Syndrome" by Ruchika Tulshyan and Jodi-Ann Bury. The article states that imposter syndrome is a problematic concept that excludes the effects of systemic misogyny, racism, and other biases in the workplace. They state that

> imposter syndrome puts the blame on individuals, without accounting for the historical and cultural contexts that are foundational to how it manifests in both women of color and white women…imposter syndrome took a fairly universal feeling of discomfort, second-guessing, and mild anxiety in the workplace and pathologized it, especially for women.[8]

When I posted a link to the article in my Facebook group, Thresette Briggs, CEO of Performance 3 LLC and a certified John C. Maxwell Coach, stated,

> Excellent article. I totally agree with the sections on the systems that perpetuate the problem, and instead of attempting to fix the

systems and understand and leverage the strengths and diverse cultures of women, especially women of color, there's a tendency to try to fix them, which only makes it worse.

Kristina Bouweiri, CEO of Reston Limousine and Founder of Sterling Women, Sterling, VA, told me that

> I had imposter syndrome for years. When I started running the company that my husband founded, I had no relevant experience, and I didn't believe I was qualified; I felt like an imposter. I didn't know how to run a business; everything I knew was what my husband had taught me. But I didn't want to run the company the same way my husband had because I didn't like how he ran it and how he treated people, so I really lacked confidence that I was doing it right.
>
> The thing that made me get over it was at a Vistage event. I was the only woman in my group, and the speaker had everyone write anonymous notes to everyone else saying how they felt about them, and one note I got said that I was the smartest person in the room. That completely changed my mindset. Then when I started Sterling Women, it was a huge success right away. It grew so quickly without me even really doing anything. That gave me the confidence to divorce my husband and buy him out of the business, and I never felt like an imposter again.

I think many leaders do have occasional imposter syndrome. Sometimes our confidence takes a hit. And sometimes, we feel unworthy or feel like a fraud. We exude confidence publicly yet question ourselves privately. That's normal. For many leaders, getting past imposter syndrome happens when they look back and see what they achieved and realized that they were truly capable after all. For others, relief comes from realizing that they are just as qualified, as smart, and as good as the other people in the room, or from realizing that the other people in the room aren't smarter or more qualified than you as you originally believed.

CHAPTER TAKEAWAYS

→ Imposter syndrome is extremely common; up to 70 percent of all adults (not just women) have had it at one time or another. Even extremely successful people get imposter syndrome. Don't let imposter syndrome stop you from pursuing your goals.

→ People with imposter syndrome often do a better job because they are more careful and conscientious than overconfident peers.

→ To get over imposter syndrome, identify and evaluate what is causing it. Do you feel like you lack the experience you need to be qualified? Some kind of educational qualification? That you're just not as smart as people think you are? Identify the specific way you think you're less qualified, and work on that. You can take a class, do extra research, or volunteer to serve in a capacity that will give you that extra experience.

→ Compare your qualifications and achievements to your peers, and you'll find that you're not as lacking as you fear. Ask your peers for feedback on how they see you; it will probably be more positive than you expect.

Chapter 3

MAINTAIN INTEGRITY

HONOR YOUR WORD AND DO THE RIGHT THING

"Do what you feel in your heart to be right—for you'll be criticized anyway."

—ELEANOR ROOSEVELT

Integrity is often considered to be the most important of all leadership qualities. It is defined as "the quality of being honest and having strong moral principles." To me, integrity means more than just being honest. It means following through on my commitments, keeping my word, and living in accordance with my values. Clearly, integrity requires a strong self-connection, just as the other mindsets we've discussed thus far do. How do you know if you're living in accordance with your values and moral principles if you never check in with yourself?

Penny Benkeser, the owner of nine Servpro franchises and a construction company in North Carolina, told me this story:

We had a job downtown a couple weeks ago, and it was a very,

very profitable job. And you know, everybody's scrapping right now. So I call in a buddy Servpro franchise owner, and I say, "I want you guys to help out. We're going to give you X amount of square footage." The job ends, everything went great, and he sends me an invoice for the square footage that I told him he was going to clean. And my ops manager came back to me and said, "Actually, they cleaned a good bit more than that." It was about fifteen thousand dollars worth of work more than we had agreed, but he'd already invoiced me. I could have just paid the invoice; he wouldn't know any better. So I sent him a text, and I told him to change his invoice, that we made an error on the square footage and he needs to up it by fifteen thousand dollars. And he sent me a text back and said, "Wow, that speaks volumes about who you are."

And I thought that it would have been so easy to pocket the fifteen thousand dollars. But it would have been dishonest. And what would my ops manager have taken from that encounter if I'd said we're not going to adjust it? Do your people want to work for you if you're dishonest? I don't think so. I think it's a reason that we have much lower turnover than the industry average. I think people trust that what we tell them we're going to do, we're going to do. And we're going to follow through. I think it is fundamental to how we do business in every aspect.

I had a mentor whom I asked years ago why he thought he's been so successful. And he said, "Because I always do the right thing. Just do the right thing—you know what it is, just do that." And so when we interview job candidates, I ask them, "Why do you want to work here?" And I hear similar responses over and over again. "You have a good reputation. You pay your subs. You pay your people. When you say you're going to do something, you do it." And it warms the cockles of my heart.

Oprah Winfrey once said, "Real integrity is doing the right thing, knowing that nobody's going to know whether you did it or not." Doing the right thing can be difficult, especially as a leader juggling multiple priorities and answering to multiple stakeholders.

Especially in the corporate world, it can be particularly difficult to work with integrity because of the focus on short-term results and financial gains. The dilemma often revolves around money, but not always. Will you take a shortcut that will result in higher profits but give the customer a lower quality product? What if your supervisor or your customer is telling you to do something that you know isn't ethical? Or promises you a promotion in exchange for pretending not to notice that they made a mistake? It's very easy to tell yourself that you'll take the shortcut or go along with the ethical lapse just this one time, and nobody will know, but as soon as you do it the first time, it's much easier to do it again, and again. And once you go down that slippery slope, you'll lose the respect and trust of the people you lead and your own self-respect.

An important exercise is to define your core values: your fundamental beliefs or guiding principles that dictate how you behave. Here again, connecting with yourself is critical. If you don't know your values, you won't know if you're operating in alignment with them. You can google "examples of core values" and get lists of dozens of values to choose from. You need to reflect on them to decide which ones are most important to you. Then decide how you will react if a situation comes up that is outside your values.

Many people espouse certain values but then don't act in integrity with those values. The author Glennon Doyle said that "integrity means there is not a real-life you and an internet you. The two are one and the same. If you're not kind on the internet, you're not kind."

Maria Gamb, the Founder of NMS Communications and author of *Values-Based Leadership for Dummies*, told me that leading based on core values is the cornerstone of how a leader should operate. She says:

A grounded way of being a leader is to understand what your values are. You can establish boundaries and rules of engagement and how you will be in the workplace, how people can rely on you to be every single day. So if you value integrity, you'd better be intact. You'd better act with integrity at all times. If you do, it's okay for you to ask your team for that commitment. And it also becomes an agreement.

We once had this issue where one of my new team members was working with one of our vendors. She was so sweet, completely well-intentioned, and she was so excited because the vendor offered her box seat tickets at the stadium. We have a company policy that you can't accept a gift over twenty-five dollars unless it's food that can be shared with the whole office. And I called her into my office because I had heard about it, and I said, "One, there's this policy, but two, and more importantly, is your integrity. The perception could be that you'll grant them favors because of the tickets." And I explained it to her, and she was horrified. I said, "Don't worry, we're having a conversation, we're not having a judgment. At the end of the day, you have to make the decision for yourself."

That's always the hard thing as a leader is you have to trust people to make the right decision. I think that when you set up your leadership around your values, you're committed to staying within those guidelines, and you lead by example. We do a formal process around let's get to your values. How are you going to convey them to your people? But it really is about living it and setting the example that you want them to follow.

I always hire people based on who they are and their potential rather than their experience. Of course, there must be experience. But I hire first based on the person and their willingness to learn, and to have integrity. I hire based on my value system.

When I served on the NAWBO National Board, we defined the core values for our board. One of those values was Integrity, and we defined it as "honest and truthful when dealing with the business of NAWBO; takes responsibility for her actions; accountable to the NAWBO Board Code of Conduct; strongly based in ethical and caring behavior; and reliable, responsible and authentic in words and actions." When interviewing applicants to the Board each year, we ask each person what integrity means to them, and we ask their references to provide examples of the person acting with integrity.

One of my personal core values is respect for all people and all work. Nothing bothers me more than people who are rude or disrespectful to restaurant servers, janitors, flight attendants, and others whom they deem to be in "lesser" type positions. My business partner and I sometimes spy at the reception desk when we have a candidate coming in for an important interview to see how the person treats the receptionist. We have not hired people who were otherwise qualified because of their lack of respect for the receptionist. We also have always been on a first-name basis with all of our employees, including interns and entry-level staff, and treat everyone with respect, no matter their position. They all have my email address and cell phone number and can contact me any time for any reason.

One of our corporate values is "employees matter." Early in the life of our company, we had an important client who constituted around 30 percent of our revenue. We were working on our second big project for the client and getting ready to start a third when I asked one of my employees on that project how things were going. Her response was, "Today's been a good day; I haven't cried at all." After I got over my shock, I probed for more information and found out that the client's project manager was regularly nasty to my employees and treated them unprofessionally, often to the point of tears. I spoke about it to the president of the client company, and when he was not interested in doing anything about it, I told him that we would honor our agreement to complete the current project to the best of our ability, but once it was complete, we would be canceling our contract. And we did. And we told our employees why we canceled the contract. We could have put the money first, but that would not have aligned with our values.

Tammy Dickerson, the CEO of The Baker Group, an event management company in Los Angeles, CA, told me why integrity is so important to her:

> I always say that my word is my bond, and my commitment is what I'm valued on. We even have a page in our proposals when we send them out to clients that talk about why do you want to do business with us as an agency, talking about our integrity, our morals, our values, what we stand for, what we believe in. And I think that it speaks volumes as a leader and as a business owner when it's really a part of your own morals and values and philosophy as a person.
>
> When I hire new employees, during the onboarding process, it's a discussion that we have. We're a small agency; I'm a very spiritual

person. So when I interview people, I really want to know who they are because we work together as a family. So it's important that we are on the same page, in terms of how we do business, how we believe in making sure that we're always communicating in team meetings and in retreats and how we deal with people, always in a very respectful way. That's really important to me.

It's also making sure that I am working with like-minded vendors, suppliers, and strategic partners. I have the conversation even more in light of what's happening in terms of civil unrest. I think it's one thing to say it, but it's something else to really demonstrate it and believe it. I really watch their actions; how they're dealing with people and interacting with people is important.

And I would say it's really been a great value because, for us, we're able to build very deep relationships with our clients, which is, knock on wood, why we have been around so long. But I think that when you build those kinds of relationships with clients, it really goes beyond just being a client or vendor or consultant. They become your friends. They want to do business with you because they want to see you succeed. They know that you also want to see them succeed. So it develops a different level of relationship. They know that they can trust you, and they value your opinion. That's where integrity plays a very strong role.

I remember a story from years ago because for many of the events that we work with we manage the complete budget. So if we're working with a client that has a half-million-dollar budget, then we're managing that, and they're feeding the money through our agency. We had a prospective client who said, "Wow, I don't know how I feel about giving you this amount of money and you managing it." I remember saying, "If you feel that way, then we should not be doing business." I think that resonated with them that if she feels that strongly about it, I respect that. But I'm not going to lose a business or personal relationship over money. It's just not worth it.

She ended up going with our firm. And we have had a very long-lasting relationship. Now I feel I can have even deeper and more open and honest conversations with people because we've developed a higher level of trust. I always like to tell people that we go beyond event planning. We always want people to have the best in terms of what they're doing.

Marilyn Hewson, former CEO of Lockheed Martin, said,

Leaders must exemplify integrity and earn the trust of their teams through their everyday actions. When you do this, you set high standards for everyone at your company. And when you do so with positive energy and enthusiasm for shared goals and purpose, you can deeply connect with your team and customers.

Nothing can torpedo a leader's career faster than a lack of integrity. Several behaviors can be used to identify someone with a lack of integrity. First, they refuse to accept responsibility for problems or mistakes and are happy to let others take the blame. They fail to meet commitments or follow through with their promises. They get defensive and refuse to apologize when called out. They say one thing and do another. They are not reliable or trustworthy. They brag and boast and don't like to share credit. They lie and tell people what they think they want to hear. They can be very manipulative to get what they want.

There are quite a few examples of Fortune 500 CEOs found to

have embellished their resumes or claimed degrees they didn't actually earn, who were fired and forfeited millions in earnings, even when they were doing a good job of running the corporation. They often claim it was an honest mistake or happened so long ago that it shouldn't matter anymore. But upon investigation, it's usually found that individuals who lie on their resumes are regularly dishonest throughout their careers.

A lack of integrity can be more subtle than being overtly dishonest. As Olalah Njenga, CEO of YellowWood Consulting and past President of the NAWBO Raleigh chapter, told me,

> Another important thing is to never sacrifice integrity for popularity. I see that in my NAWBO chapter, and I have seen that in my chapter's history of leadership, where it was more important to be popular and be liked, even if they had to skirt the fringes of integrity. But they forgot that being liked is not the same as being respected. And I had to say to one of our leaders that we have very different leadership styles, and the difference is that I would rather be respected, and you would rather be liked.

> I think that is the crux of what keeps women from being great leaders instead of simply good leaders. It reminds me of the quote: "The difference between a good leader and a great leader is a good leader knows when to say yes, and a great leader knows when to say no." And I think this is what trips women up because we are socialized to say yes, as often as we can. And there's a time to say no. For me as a leader, the time to say no is when it is not in alignment with integrity. And so, I see women leaders constantly compromising little pieces of their integrity for popularity. I'm just not that girl. I'm the girl that raises her hand and says, "I don't think that's going to work" when everybody else is like, "Yes, let's do it."

CHAPTER TAKEAWAYS

→ There is value in taking time to reflect, consider, and write down your personal values in all aspects of your life. When you write ideas down, you will find that you think about them more deeply.

→ Think about your personal values around how you will conduct your life. Integrity is about more than just being honest—it means honoring your commitments and living daily in accordance with your core values.

→ Think about your business ethics around how you relate to clients, subcontractors, and employees. Employee respect and appreciation should be carefully stated and followed as your employees are at the heart of your business and life.

→ Your integrity is the most effective way to build trust with your employees, customers, vendors, and colleagues.

→ Nothing can destroy your reputation faster than a lack of integrity; if you make a mistake, you can fix it, but if you're perceived to be dishonest or lack integrity, you will be forever mistrusted.

Chapter 4

GAIN CONFIDENCE

BELIEVE IN YOUR LEADERSHIP ABILITIES

"People respond well to those who are sure of what they want."

—ANNA WINTOUR

When Diana and I first founded our company, I had zero sales experience. Every job I had ever had was either doing the work or managing the people doing the work. Never bringing in the work. About a week after starting the company, we got an opportunity to meet with the owner of a small business that was trying to break into the government market. Unfortunately, Diana couldn't make the meeting, so I had to go by myself.

I was really nervous, so for several days before the meeting, Diana and I spent hours putting together a PowerPoint deck outlining the various services we could provide, coming up with a script, and practicing what I would say until I was pretty sure I could handle it. The day came, I got to the meeting, and one of the people from the company flipped through the deck, pulled out one or two slides, turned the rest over on the table, and said, "Tell me about these."

Everything I had practiced for the last few days was out the window. I stumbled through an explanation of the services, then the owner outlined a project in that area and asked me how much we would charge. I froze. Diana and I hadn't really talked about pricing. I made up a number on the spot.

We didn't get the job—not because the price I came up with was too much, but because I was a nervous wreck the whole time and didn't project confidence in our ability to do the project. They didn't want to work with someone so unsure of themselves and the value they brought, and I didn't blame them. Truthfully, given that we had never done a project like that, as our business was only a week old, I wasn't confident in our abilities.

Diana had had plenty of previous business development experience and was much more comfortable in that role, so for the first few months, I let her take the lead in meetings with potential clients and watched how she responded to questions and how she generally handled herself. I was good at talking about the work we could do, but she had to do the sales-y part and discuss why we were the right company to work with and ask for the business. After a while, I got more comfortable in those kinds of meetings, and over the years, I brought in a lot more business than she did because I got very confident in the benefits we offer, the quality of work we produce, and the value we provide.

One of the things that people often mention when asked about the characteristics of great leaders is charisma. What is charisma really? It's the aura of someone who is comfortable in their own skin, who knows that they have something to offer, and who is confident in themselves, their goals, their identity, and their vision.

Confidence may not be the most important mindset for someone to master to be an effective leader, but it *is* the attribute that most causes other people to follow them. Think about it, who would you most want to work for? A boss who hems and haws and doesn't seem sure of themselves or what they want? Or someone who knows what they want and puts it out there confidently? I think all of us would choose the latter.

Effective leaders project confidence. They understand their strengths and can communicate their vision. Does this mean they always are 100 percent sure of themselves? Very few people are always 100 percent sure of themselves, but effective leaders have learned to project that image.

Some people seem to be born with a lot of self-confidence, but for the rest of the world, developing confidence in yourself is not always easy. This will be yet another exercise in self-connection. How you think has a direct correlation to how you lead. Again, if you wouldn't want to work for a leader lacking confidence, it's highly probable that your employees don't want to work for someone lacking confidence as well.

Lisa Hickey, a John Maxwell–certified leadership coach, explained that "being confident is the biggest weapon you can have when you're trying to be on equal footing with men or even with other accomplished women. You have to have that."

You can have confidence and also be humble (which we'll talk more about in Chapter 13). Having confidence doesn't mean being egotistical, conceited, or boastful. Melanie Thomas Armstrong, a former partner at Arthur Andersen, PricewaterhouseCoopers

(PwC), and Guidehouse, told me this story about when she was a junior manager and was struggling with confidence:

> I had the office next to Ira [a senior partner]. I had just brought in a million-dollar project. Drew (a senior manager) goes running down the hall with a bottle of champagne, goes to Ira's office, pops it. And they're celebrating because he won a hundred-thousand-dollar project. And I was sitting in my office thinking, *Are you kidding me? They're popping champagne for a hundred-thousand-dollar job. I just signed a million.* And then I thought, *Oh my God, Ira isn't celebrating me because he doesn't know about it. Because I didn't tell him.* I just expected him to know.

> To me, that changed everything in my career because then I found ways to tell people what I had accomplished without feeling like I was bragging. That was a very big moment for me to change the way I interacted and that I made sure people knew what I was doing. It was moments like that which gave me the confidence to think, *I do belong here.*

There are some actions you can take to develop more self-confidence. First, go back and read Chapter 1 about mental chatter and recalibrate the voice in your head to focus on your positive attributes and strengths. If Stan is constantly telling you that you're stupid, lazy, or incompetent, it's going to be impossible to be confident in yourself.

Second, set some small goals and try to achieve them. If you don't achieve them, analyze what went wrong and make corrections to achieve them the next time you try. Then set goals that are slightly bigger and achieve those. Then make them bigger. Then bigger still. Each time you reach your goals, you gain confidence that you can do it again and even better next time. For example, if you decided to run a marathon, you would start training by running a mile for a few days in a row. Then run two miles. You gradually increase the distance you can run at one time, first doing a 5K, then a 10K, then a 10-miler. If the first time you ran, you tried to do ten miles, the likelihood of success would be slim, and you wouldn't be able to walk for a week afterward. It's the same with all big goals. You have to work up to them, gaining more confidence at each level. By the time you've done a few 10Ks, a 5K is no big deal.

Jenni Romanek, the Director of Analytics at Instagram, told me,

> I do feel like I've built a lot of confidence over the last couple of years in my leadership. A big part of how I did that was failure and then coming back from failure. When I first started my role at Instagram, I remember feeling deeply insecure and that incredible imposter syndrome that we talked about. In my first month or two on the job, I was really nervous about doing a good job. I did well, but I also had some failures early on, as was natural to expect because there were things I didn't know how to do, or I made wrong choices, and I didn't ask for help when I needed it. But having a couple of those failures shook me to where I realized I had to do some things differently. And those were the incredible growth spurts that I had as a leader. And so I hope that others can recognize, too, the fertile time for growth is not when things are going well—it's when things aren't going well—and to seize that time and to really ask what's going wrong and why.

> Getting into the why is, I think, the richest part, and that's the part that goes beyond just the professional but also to the personal kind of inner work. Figuring out what's driving me and what behaviors or these fears are holding me back. And in my case, I didn't want

to screw things up again. So whenever those setbacks occurred, I would come up with a tactical plan of how I would do things differently the next time. And that worked. Each time, I felt like the next time it went better, and I was getting positive feedback. And that was fueling more growth and taking on challenges that felt a little bit uncomfortable. I always try to make sure that I have at least something on my plate, some projects, or new team I'm taking on that makes me uncomfortable because if I'm not feeling a little bit uncomfortable I'm probably not pushing myself enough. It's been really rewarding to see as I've taken on more projects that make me uncomfortable that I've continued to be able to do them. Certainly not flawlessly, certainly not perfectly, but that's not a standard that I'm holding myself to. I think it's continued to build confidence by taking difficult things on and seeing that I can do it, and then taking on the next challenge. My advice to other women is get a little uncomfortable. Don't get into the danger zone where you feel like you have no idea what you're doing, and you're stuck. But definitely get into that learning discomfort zone. And recognize that if you're feeling too comfortable with how things are going, it might be worth shaking it up a little bit.

Another way to boost your self-confidence is to help someone else. It may not sound logical, but helping others makes you feel better about yourself. Be kind to someone who is struggling, hold the door for the mom with two toddlers trying to get out of the grocery store, buy a stranger's coffee at Starbucks, or volunteer for a charity or cause you believe in.

You can also build your confidence by being secure in your physical appearance. I'm not saying to get Botox or that you have to have the body of a supermodel in order to be confident, not at all. But being happy with how you look helps. When you're in a situation where you want to project confidence, make sure you're well-groomed, and your clothes are clean and appropriate for the situation. Or, as Mel Robbins describes in her book, give yourself a high five in the mirror every morning, and you'll start looking forward to seeing yourself and feeling positive about it instead of negative.

One popular trick to give yourself a boost of confidence in a moment of uncertainty is to do the Wonder Woman stance. Stand up tall, put your hands on your waist, stick your chest out, and hold your head high. Hold that stance for thirty seconds, and you'll feel stronger and braver and have the confidence to face your challenges. One woman I know lifts weights in the morning, before she gives a speech, to show herself how strong she is.

You don't have to have the charisma of Michelle Obama in order to be a confident leader. You do need to be secure in who you are and what you bring to the table. Because if you don't believe that you're worth following, nobody else will think so either. As Beyoncé once said, "The most alluring thing a woman can have is confidence."

CHAPTER TAKEAWAYS

→ Confidence is the key attribute that attracts people to you. If you don't believe you're worth following, nobody else will either.

→ To gain confidence, make sure Stan is telling you how great you are (go back and read Chapter 1 again). Then set some small goals. Once you achieve them, set bigger goals, and achieve those.

→ Make a list of your strengths. Acknowledge and be confident in them.

→ Make a list of your weaknesses. Identify a plan to improve on those areas and turn them into strengths.

→ Another way to increase your confidence is to help others. Teach a workshop, volunteer for a charity, or perform random acts of kindness.

Chapter 5

BE DECISIVE

STOP WAFFLING AND MAKE A DECISION

"Indecision is the most unsexy thing on the planet."

—DREW BARRYMORE

When I worked at Arthur Andersen, I had a boss named Jack Summers who had a powerful method of breaking logjams. If we were waiting for instructions from a partner about which direction to take on a project or what to tell a client and the partner wasn't being responsive, Jack would send a "UNODIR" (pronounced "you know dear") email. UNODIR was short for "unless otherwise directed," and the email would say something like, "The deadline is tomorrow, and I haven't heard from you, so unless otherwise directed, here's what I'm going to do..." The vast majority of the time, the partner would respond that that was fine, to go ahead. Occasionally they would answer and say to do something different, and sometimes they wouldn't respond at all because they concurred with the proposed action.

Over time, I learned that the beauty of UNODIR is two-fold: not only does it get things moving, but it also strengthens your relationship with the boss or client because the action you plan to take has to be a good one. If you say, "UNODIR, I'm going to blow this up," then the boss or client who reads the email will freak out and scramble to stop you from setting the explosion. And if that happens more than once, they will lose confidence in your decision-making skills and in you. But when your proposed actions are the right ones, the boss or client respects your decision-making abilities and trusts you more.

Being decisive is of the utmost importance for an effective leader because, by definition, leadership decisions are important decisions. Decisions that aren't important should be delegated down—deciding what brand of copier paper to buy is not worth the leader's time, which needs to be spent making decisions of consequence.

Lynda Bishop, Vice President of Programs for the NAWBO Institute, told me about the importance of decisiveness in one of her previous jobs:

> I was in a very male-dominated industry as one of the few female leaders, so decisiveness was important. It could have been the role that I was in or the particular industry, but often I didn't have a lot of time to really weigh things or take my time to think about it or collaborate with other people before making a decision. So one of the things that they looked to me to do was to be able to make a decision and stick to it and push forward. Had I waffled on anything, I would have lost the respect and the confidence people had in me.
>
> My decisiveness was closely related to my integrity because part of what they knew they could count on me for was to make decisions

based on the right thing to do, based on my value system. This was not always the same thing as what they wanted me to do because integrity was something that they struggled with, which is why I left that organization.

I knew that they counted on me for both my decisiveness and my integrity because their values were very much more about them themselves and the finances and how much money they thought they could make. They knew if they brought it to me, I would quickly look at it and determine whether or not this was good for people, if it was the right thing to do for our customers, for our sales team, and how did it all go together. Because I always looked at everything through the human quotient of what does this actually mean and how will this affect real people.

I would make my decisions based on much more than the finances. Then I would stick to it. I was the person that held their feet to the fire on those things, which didn't always make me popular. But when I combined it with confidence, saying, "I'm sure this is the right thing, and I'm willing to stand on it," then they made better decisions. They didn't always go with mine, but a lot of times, they would at least find a compromise so that they would make better decisions for the long run.

Lesa Seibert, the CEO of Mightily, an advertising agency in Louisville, KY, agreed. She said,

In growing my business over the last several years and then talking to other women business owners, I keep hearing them say that they don't know if they're doing the right things; they're not sure if this is the way they should go. I'm totally guilty of that myself. What I found is that in most cases where I've been indecisive and second-guessed myself, it was the wrong thing to do. If I had just stayed the course and done what I had initially planned to do, it would have been a much better path forward. And in some cases, it resulted in not getting something versus getting something because of being indecisive. So I think, as long as you do your homework and you've researched whatever it is, decide what path you want to take forward, then just do it. Don't sit there worrying about it or wondering is it the right thing/is it not the right thing? And you end up missing out on opportunities that may not come along again.

I have learned the hard way to quit second-guessing myself and just know that you know what you know. I know that sounds funny, but just trust yourself to go forward. We all fail at times, and you learn from those and fail forward and don't make that mistake again.

Although decisiveness comes naturally to some, and some are better at it than others, the good news is that with practice and the right tools, leaders can develop their mindsets to improve their decision-making abilities.

Olalah Njenga, CEO of YellowWood Consulting in Raleigh, NC, talked to me about the importance of learning to be more decisive. She said,

Decisiveness is a muscle. The more you use it, the better you get at it. I think oftentimes, when women are decisive, they get shamed for it. And they get called names. And so, they tend to shy away from decision-making and lean toward the validation of the peer group.

So one of the things that I tried to explain to those women is you may never get comfortable with it, but you have to make being decisive familiar to you. So you need to think of being decisive as a coat that you put on. So every opportunity you get to put on that coat, it's about making the coat feel familiar because, at the end of the day, you are the leader.

You are responsible for the weight of the result of the decision. No one else can carry it for you. If you invite a bunch of people in so you can get a consensus about a decision, and then it goes wrong, those people have scattered because they have no skin in the game. Not only do you have a big invoice for me to help you course-correct and undo the stuff that everybody told you was a good idea, but nobody is there to help you deal with the fallout.

So how do you learn to be more decisive? There is a proven process that you should follow when making important decisions. The process is: gather information about the subject matter, identify the desired outcome, review and analyze the options, weigh the possible outcomes, and choose. Do not skip any step of that process because each is important.

First, leaders should be as informed as necessary, depending on the situation. The more important the circumstances, the more information is required. However, there is no situation where the leader will have *all* of the possibly relevant data. And depending on the urgency of the situation, they must often make decisions with imperfect information. Do not let that stop you from making a decision altogether.

Lisa Rosenthal, CEO of Mayvin, a Defense contracting firm in Annandale, VA, says the best way to make solid decisions is to "listen to those that are advising you. Surround yourself with a Team of Rivals that will challenge you. It is absolutely okay to be wrong, but it is not okay to not listen before making a decision."

Melanie Thomas Armstrong, a former partner at Arthur Andersen, PricewaterhouseCoopers, and Guidehouse, told me that

> women leaders cannot be wishy-washy. You need to assess what information is available right now, and, based on that, make a decision. If it's wrong, then fix it later.

> If you wait until you can see all the information, you don't look thoughtful; you seem wishy-washy. I'm very comfortable making a decision based on the information available to me right now. I don't feel the need to wait three weeks for more information.

> I think that's a key characteristic that women need to have in order to be effective. I'm thinking about all the women in our leadership group. Every one of them is super competent. Super smart. It's not like they're making a bunch of crappy decisions. They're making good decisions. Maybe there could have been a slightly better one occasionally, but is it worth that maybe 5 percent extra goodness of the decision for the extra time and energy it would take?

> And you know, we have to be super competent. We have to get good at everything. If you take more time with decisions, it will be more thoughtful, and you will have gathered more information. But it will take much longer. Men can get away with that. We can't get away with that because then we're not accomplishing the seventeen other things that have to get done.

Once you have collected the available information, identify the desired outcome. What is the result you're hoping for? Next, look at the options for action. It's rare for a decision to have only two possible options, but it's often presented that way. Yes or no? Up or down? When one of your people brings the problem to you, always ask them to present at least three options to resolve the problem and identify which one they recommend and why. If none of their options are the right one, you as the leader need to identify other options that they may not have thought of.

Then, weigh the possible outcomes. Many people avoid making decisions because they fear that others may be unhappy about the decision. It might make the leader unpopular or disliked. They're afraid that they will make the wrong decision and look bad, or it will have detrimental effects on the organization. Those are all possible outcomes, so effective leaders must focus on the most likely option to achieve the desired outcome, regardless of its popularity or how others may react.

Finally, make a choice and stand by it. A leader who can't or won't make a decision, who waffles or flip-flops, loses the respect of their clients, superiors, and employees.

Jennifer Peek, the CEO of Peek Advisory Group in Kansas City, MO, shared her viewpoint:

> Regarding decisiveness, I have found that either you make the decision and you implement it, or you end up thinking about making the decision over and over and over and over again. I mean, not deciding is a decision, but it is such an energy drain. You just keep thinking and thinking and thinking and thinking. The other thing is, particularly as women business leaders, we have to make a lot of decisions all of the time. And the better

you become at flexing your decision muscle, the better it is. And it also provides this level of clarity about how you lead, how you want your business to show up, what direction you're taking it, and honestly, what decisions you're not available for.

When I first started my business, I had to make a lot of decisions all of the time because it wasn't clear to the team what they were supposed to be doing. So once you clarify it, you don't have to make the decisions anymore. Also, when I first started, we did a much broader set of work. It was still related to our offerings, but it was broader. I'll give you an example. We would do business valuations for estate planning or divorces. There's a lot of different reasons that you might need a business valuation. And I decided we're not going to do that anymore. We're really going to focus on mergers and acquisitions and the elements that support that.

And so that narrows down all of the expert knowledge. It helps narrow down who your network needs to be, what you focus on in your marketing. All of those things. So that one decision eliminated the need for a whole bunch of future decisions. I think in those moments when I was making some of those decisions, I was worried that I was cutting myself off—I'm going to have to turn away clients. But it did turn out to be better in the end, in the long run.

And the other thing about it is that we have historically gotten 90 percent of our business from referrals from other professional service providers, and now it's easier for them to talk about us. Because we do one thing. And I think that makes a big difference because they don't have to say, "They do this, and they do that and this other thing." Making that tough decision changed my business.

If it turns out that your information was incomplete or your analysis of the outcome was incorrect, and the decision was a mistake, then be honest and transparent and make it right. Everyone makes bad calls now and then; it's how you handle it after the fact that matters. There are tons of stories of leaders who make a bad decision, realize it, apologize, and fix the problem. There are also tons of stories of leaders who make a bad decision, realize it, lie about it or try to justify it, and have it blow up in their faces. Google "United Airlines dragging passenger off the plane" for a prime example.

Jenni Romanek, Director of Analytics at Instagram, agrees. She said,

> I think that an early challenge for me in developing my own leadership and leading teams was feeling like I always had to make the right decisions. Especially when you're leading teams, a decision is always better than no decision. And the worst thing you can do as a leader is to waffle or be ambiguous in your language or be unwilling to make calls. And leaders always make wrong calls. Leaders always make bad decisions, and you have to sign up for that.
>
> If you want to take on a leadership role, you have to be willing to live with the consequences, but also know that not making a decision is almost uniformly always worse. And people understand if you explain why you've made a decision at the time that you're making it—and it later turns out that that's not right—as long as you've been really clear about the why and it's a firm rationale. Even if there are other rationales that could be true, too, they'll understand. I think building that skill of decisiveness requires getting comfortable with vulnerability because making a decision

is a vulnerable act. It's an act of courage, and it means accepting that you could be wrong. I often try to describe it to folks on my team as risk-taking. You have to have some appetite for risk-taking if you want to be a leader because you have to be willing to make choices that are potentially wrong and some that are going to be wrong.

In her MasterClass, "Learn How to Be a Boss," Anna Wintour states,

Worrying about what others might think can dilute your judgment and your effectiveness and be disruptive to your leadership and your decision-making. Trust yourself to own your choices, don't bow to consensus or pressure to follow other peoples' way of thinking or looking at things. There are going to be moments in your career when you make mistakes. It's super important to own those mistakes and then to move forward.

Whether decisiveness comes easily to you, or you find it difficult, it's super important to understand that women leaders need to be decisive to be respected. Learning to make solid decisions quickly and stand by them is one of the most important things a leader does.

CHAPTER TAKEAWAYS

→ Leadership decisions are important decisions. If a decision isn't important, delegate it.

→ Not making a decision is a decision.

→ Men are often given slack if they waffle or are wishy-washy, but indecisive women lose the respect of their boss, clients, and followers.

→ To get comfortable making decisions, look for choices about things that aren't life or death so you get used to flexing your decision-making muscle before you have to make the really important decisions.

→ You will never have 100 percent of the information needed to make the best decision; sometimes, you have to accept that the information you have is enough and go with it.

→ Making a wrong decision isn't the end of the world; if you make a mistake, you earn respect by admitting it and fixing the problem.

Chapter 6

CULTIVATE RESILIENCE

GET KNOCKED DOWN AND GET BACK UP

"I really think a champion is defined not by their wins but by how they can recover when they fail."

—SERENA WILLIAMS

In 2008, about seven years after Diana and I started our business, the economy crashed. Our biggest customer filed for bankruptcy, owing us a quarter-million dollars that we knew we would never see a dime of. We had to figure out what to do and how we would stay afloat. We had ten employees who depended on us for their livelihoods.

We discussed whether we should shut down the company or keep going. We decided we were going to fight through it and do everything in our power to keep the business going. At that time, we were doing consulting work for small businesses, and we decided that we were going to start bidding on government contracts. It took quite a while before we got our first contract and transitioned the company away from the small consulting jobs and into the longer-term government contracts. We went without paying ourselves for several months, but we never missed a payroll for our employees and didn't lay off anyone. Six years later, we made the Inc. 5000 list for the first time.

Resilience—sometimes referred to as "grit"—is the ability to keep going when times are hard. So many people quit when faced with difficult circumstances, but if you want to be an effective leader, you need to be able to bounce back. That doesn't necessarily mean to keep doing what you were doing if that wasn't successful. Instead, shift your mindset to see the setback not as a failure, but as a learning opportunity.

It would have been easier for Diana and me to have given up and shut down the company when things got tough. But we decided that we would bounce back, keep pushing, and make it work. When things are tough, you need a mindset of resilience the most. It allows you to find the strength to continue on.

Lisa Rosenthal, CEO of Mayvin, a Defense contracting firm in Annandale, VA, said,

> When we started Mayvin thirteen years ago, none of the original owners had ever been managers, leaders, or corporate executives. We only had a passion for learning and treating people well. We failed early, and we failed often, and I don't regret any of our mistakes because we keep learning from them. We listened to hear what we were doing right and, most importantly, what we were doing wrong. I never thought we would surpass one million per year. Today we are in over twenty states and well over fifty million in revenue!

When Sara Blakely tells the story of the founding of Spanx, she talks about having the idea to cut the feet off a pair of pantyhose so her butt would look better in her pants and she could still wear cute sandals. When she decided to start a company to sell these, she contacted every hosiery mill in the United States, and not a single one was willing to work with her to produce her product. She didn't give up, and eventually, one mill owner agreed to make them after his daughters told him what a brilliant idea it was. She decided to patent the idea. Every single law firm she talked to about filing a patent thought it was crazy and wanted to charge her thousands of dollars. She didn't have the money, so she bought a book to learn the process and filed for the patent herself. No matter what obstacle or setback she encountered, she believed in herself and her idea, and she kept pushing. We all know how the story ends; she became the youngest self-made female billionaire in US history.

Penny Benkeser, who owns nine Servpro franchises and a construction company in North Carolina, talked about the importance of resilience in business and in life. She said,

> If you can teach your children nothing more than to be resilient, then you rock the house. I just don't think there's a choice. When you get knocked down, the only choice is to rise again. I mean, it's never a choice to sit it out. It's never a choice to give up. I think part of resiliency is understanding that there are always more options. For me, resilience is understanding that things are going to happen, and it's not about what happens. It's about what you do about it, and what you do is understand that there are always more options.

> If you ever get to the point in any situation where you feel like you're at your last option, then phone a friend, go somewhere, call somebody; they will show you that there are other options. If you

get to that black place where you think you've exhausted all the possibilities—no, you haven't. There are always other possibilities, and I think that helps you to be more resilient if you just say, okay, I'm at option one, but there's probably fifty more. That's what gives me the motivation to keep going. You just keep looking for other alternatives. I just think that not standing up again after you get knocked down is not an option.

Jessica Billingsley, CEO of Akerna, a Denver software company that serves the cannabis industry, told me,

From very early on, I was in the camp that if you tell me not to do something, I'm going to figure out a way to do it. I grew up in Georgia before the launch of STEM initiatives for girls. I'm a woman CEO in tech, and in cannabis, and now publicly traded. There are no others at this moment in time that are at that intersection. I'm at the leading edge of the leading edge.

I'm a rock climber, and there are some interesting parallels in terms of making judicious decisions, being willing to take the risks, but then also facing the consequence of falls. And it comes down to mental grit, to that mental grit, problem-solving, and just sheer will, sheer determination. I get knocked down, but I get up again.

I want to share something that I experienced in the early days and founding of our company. In 2011, as a new SaaS company, after experiencing 800 percent year over year growth in revenue, we were turned down for equity financing, and I mean turned down by everyone. We had several very promising term sheets. So we got to term sheet phase, which generally closes in this world because they're fairly competitive. What would happen is we would sign these term sheets, and then we would get further into definitive documents, and somebody, the attorney or accountant, would pull the plug and shut the investment down due to the ancillary relationship to cannabis. I was left with few options. I had already forgone a salary for a year and a half. And, frankly, I had gotten divorced and had custody of my daughter and breadwinner responsibility. I had to make some decisions.

I'm unusually risk-tolerant, and I could see what we were doing, and I could see the growth trajectory. And I decided I truly believed in the company's mission and growth prospects, and I took out loans that I signed for personally to continue the company's operations. That gamble paid off. I was successful and turned the company profitable by the next year in record time, even without the outside funding. I paid back all those loans by the next year. So we did ultimately take outside financing at a time when we were profitable as a company the following year, but it was from a different place and a different mindset. In doing that at a later time, having taken that risk, I was able to retain more ownership.

I just knew in the back of my mind, in six months, I'll either be done, or I'll be doing this very well, and I know I lived years of my life that way. I think there's a certain tolerance level for risk that is required in the leader. I don't think that's gender-related, but I think there is a necessity in a leader to have a high tolerance for ambiguity and risk because you're literally making it up as you go along. I think that's particularly hard for women because I think that there is a theme of perfection. You're not trying something unless you know that you can succeed. Being willing to "fail forward" and being willing to get into a place of resilience, I think, is very important. So first, it means you need to try, right? And after you try, then you can actually reach somewhere. So if you fail, then you have to be willing to try again. And that's a bit of a mindset and a bit of a mind shift. Something that we can do, we can work on.

There's a popular story about Thomas Edison, the inventor of the light bulb. He famously made ten thousand different prototypes of the light bulb, and none of them worked. When he finally made a prototype that worked, he was asked how he had kept going after failing ten thousand times. His response was that he hadn't failed ten thousand times; instead, he had identified ten thousand ways that didn't work.

The COVID-19 pandemic caused a lot of businesses to struggle. As a result, resilience was something that many leaders had to call on. Tammy Dickerson, CEO of The Baker Group, an event management company in Los Angeles, CA, told me about how she needed resilience to keep moving after the pandemic struck in 2020:

> Our business is down by more than 50 percent with the pandemic, needless to say with live events, but we've looked at this new environment in terms of virtual events, and we're pivoting, and now that's what we're focusing on. So it was a whole new skillset that we're learning, which has been pretty exciting.
>
> But it was either that we're going to go out of business, or we're going to change and flip the script and do something different. And I think that after we had our pity party, we said, "Okay, this is where we are. We're going to be here for a minute. So how do we pick up, keep it moving, keep it pushing, and look at what our next steps are." So I think resilience is really important because you have to be able to shake it off.
>
> We've all been down and out. There are good days, there are bad days,

but what I've learned is to just keep moving and doing something. I used to feel like it was all about the big things, but now I've gotten to a place where I think it's about the small things and giving yourself credit for the small things. I think we tend to beat ourselves up when we don't do them, but it's okay to say, "You know what? I actually did two emails today, and I feel really good about those two emails."

It's all about just doing a little something every day, continuing to push forward, continuing to believe in the strength that we have. Continue to be positive and optimistic and to allow ourselves to have a bad day, but just to get up the next day with a new mindset.

We're all going to get pretty beat up in a lot of different ways. I remember when I left Coca-Cola, and I started my business, one of my managers told me, "You think that you worked hard at Coke? You're going to work ten times harder for yourself." And I have. But it's been worth it, and I wouldn't change a thing. And I don't think I could've done it without being resilient.

Jeanette Armbrust, the Managing Director of Skyline Exhibits of Greater LA, a company that makes exhibit booths for trade shows, agreed that resilience has been necessary since the pandemic started. She relates,

When COVID hit, my business crashed, a half-million dollars in contracts were canceled. At the time, I was like, "This can't get any worse." But it's gotten worse. And yet now we're retooling. What else can we do?

We know what we can't do, so we have to figure out what we can do. I think that's what it means to be resilient. It's not to just sit there and go, "This sucks." It's like, "Okay, this sucks, now what are we going to do about it?" Because if you give up, you give up. You have to figure out how to move forward. You have to be able to pivot. If you're going to be a business owner and you're going to be a leader, you better be resilient. If you get punched or knocked down, you better get back up because it's not all rainbows and glitter. Sometimes you get punched down on a daily basis, and you have to learn how to brush it off and get back in the game because if you don't, somebody else will.

Like Edison, effective leaders don't take a setback as failure; they see it as an opportunity to learn what doesn't work and try something different. For example, you launched a new product, and it bombed. Does that mean you shut down the business entirely? No. It means you figure out why the product bombed and use that information to either fix the product or come up with something new that doesn't have the same weaknesses.

I'm not saying you can't be upset that the project/product/idea failed. You absolutely can and should take some time to be sad about it. But you can't let yourself spend the next month on the couch watching *Bridgerton* with Ben & Jerry's. One approach is to give yourself a time limit to wallow. Depending on the situation, it might be for two weeks, or two days, or two hours. Either way, when the time is up, stop wallowing, and figure out what you're going to do next.

Once you've had some distance, you can rationally assess the situation, develop strategies to address the issues, and implement your plan to either fix the problem or try something new. You don't have to do it alone; engage your team to analyze the situation and brainstorm solutions. And rely on friends and family to keep your spirits up and not let you wallow more than your allotted time.

Jennifer Urezzio, the Founder of Soul Language, agreed. She told me,

> I think resilience is really important. I think when women leaders have a big vision, they naturally assume that everyone's going to get on board with that vision. When I started Soul Language, I kept talking to gurus because I really thought this was a tool for them; they're going to love this tool. But they didn't recognize the value, and I realized I was going to the wrong people. I need to go to the explorers—the people who want to experience new stuff. I found my community. So I often think when women get knocked down, they internalize it as, *Oh my God, there's something I did wrong, I failed, there must be something wrong with me.* But no, it's just about tweaking; it just means that you're off the mark. I do something called conscious evaluation where I go through and evaluate, *Okay, what worked, what didn't work, what did I learn, what can I change around?* So I can go out of the next gate with the understanding that I was off the mark, not a failure.

As I was working on this chapter, I posed the question in my Facebook group: "Is resilience a mindset or a skill?" It sparked a heated discussion, but the final consensus was that it's both. As one person said,

> A resilient mindset is one that does not accept a setback as a final answer, one that seeks the positives and the lessons within the negative. Resilience skills are the ability to logically assess situations, develop strategies and plans to address issues, obstacles, and failures, and then implement them. With this mindset and these skills, you are resilient enough to survive. When the mindset and the skills are both present and aligned, your resilience becomes supercharged. You are no longer facing obstacles and failures;

you are learning and growing. With both of these present, you are resilient enough to thrive.

Maria Gamb, the Founder of NMS Communications, had this to say about resilience:

I wrote a book called *The Resiliency Journal* for Barnes & Noble. It was a highly researched journal. They wanted the science. They wanted proof. It was very interesting. And they allowed me to temper the research with spiritual wisdom and different belief systems around resiliency.

Why is it super important that women be able to bounce back when dealing with hardships and failures? I think that women have to develop resiliency in the workplace. They're resilient mothers; they're resilient partners; they're resilient. They're taking care of their home and their family. And somewhere along the lines, they were told that they weren't resilient when it came to work, and they weren't strong enough. And I really wish that women would just stop listening to all of this noise and just do what they want to do.

If you want to be tough and you want to be resilient, then you have to keep getting up. You just have to keep getting up. I think it's Aaron Sorkin who said, "The world doesn't care how many times you fall down, as long as it's one fewer than the number of times you get back up." That's it. You just have to keep going, and that's it. And if women really would analyze their life, they would realize they're doing this all the time.

One of the keys to resilience is to have gratitude. So resilience is understanding that you not only get back up and that you keep moving on, but it's understanding that everything is a lesson and part of your journey and your development. If you fell down or you were called out because you made a mistake in your workplace, rather than sitting in shame and wanting to sulk, you need to think about what you learned from the situation. How can you do it better?

We all get redos. Life is a redo. It is. Otherwise, we would have been dead when we were six years old. So it is about learning that there is a lesson in everything. And what can you learn? What can you learn about yourself? What can you learn about the situation in terms of the skills that you need? And what could you have done better? But even more important is to have gratitude, gratitude for the experience, gratitude for the lesson; even if it's painful, you need to always be grateful.

CHAPTER TAKEAWAYS

→ Resilience is the ability to keep going after a failure, to get back up after you've been knocked down.

→ Persevering doesn't necessarily mean doing the same thing, but rather, assessing what you learned from the failure, making changes as necessary, and trying again.

→ Failure is not the end of the process; it's figuring out what didn't work and using that information to try again with a different approach.

→ There are always other options. Keep looking for other alternatives.

Chapter 7

ESTABLISH A GROWTH MINDSET

BE A PERPETUAL LEARNER

"I don't love studying. I hate studying. I like learning. Learning is beautiful."

—NATALIE PORTMAN

Since I first learned to read at age three, I have been a voracious reader. As a kid, I devoured books, starting with the Bobbsey Twins and Nancy Drew before graduating to Judy Blume, then Agatha Christie, and many others. As an adult, I still read constantly, both fiction and nonfiction. In addition to thrillers by authors like John Grisham, Lee Child, and Taylor Stevens, I read literary fiction, biographies, history, business books, memoirs, and personal development books. My entire house is filled with bookshelves crammed with books. That doesn't even count the hundreds in my Kindle and Audible accounts. Books have always been a major part of my life, and I read an average of two books a week.

I also take workshops and classes, and I regularly try new activities. I took a drawing class from the local Arts League, and while I'm not very good, I enjoyed learning a new way to express myself artistically. A few years ago, I started kayaking, and now I host monthly kayak outings on the Potomac River for my Meetup group. I also recently learned how to play pickleball and play twice a week with several friends. Even though it's been a few decades since I finished school, I always want to be learning something new.

A study conducted in 2019 by the Pew Research Center[9] discovered that approximately 27 percent of all adults in the United States hadn't read a single book in the previous year. This included print, electronic, and audiobooks. The same study found that another 43 percent had read between one and ten books the previous year, with only 29 percent of adults reading more than ten books in a year.

President Harry Truman once said, "Not all readers are leaders, but all leaders are readers." If you read just one book a month, that automatically puts you ahead of 70 percent of the population. And with around a million new books published every year in the US alone, you can find something to read on almost any topic you want to learn about.

Carol Dweck's book *Mindset* defines two types of mindsets: people with a growth mindset believe that intelligence and abilities can be developed through effort, persistence, trying different strategies, and learning from mistakes; while people with a fixed mindset believe that individuals are born with certain talents and intelligence that are fixed and unchangeable. For example, someone with a fixed mindset may think, *I'm not good at painting* and assume that will not change, while someone with a growth mindset will think, *I'm not good at painting yet* because they understand that they will get better as they practice more.

Can you see how drastically a growth mindset will affect your leadership abilities? Those with a growth mindset also have an internal fortitude, self-understanding, and connection completely foreign to those with a fixed mindset. If, as a leader, you can develop this mindset, you will be setting the example for those you are leading.

Kristina Bouweiri, CEO of Reston Limousine and the Founder of Sterling Women, agrees. She told me,

> I believe it's so important to continue to learn new things. Participation in a mastermind or other peer network group is vital. I have learned so much from my Vistage group, even more from the other members than I do from the speakers, just hearing about their challenges and how they address them. I learn new processes and strategies that I can turn around and apply in my business.

Developing a growth mindset is essential to success in today's business world of constant change and innovation. Effective leaders must also have a growth mindset; they understand that they can improve through practice, make progress through trial and error, and learn new ideas and skills, even as adults. Leaders need to be open to learning new ideas, approaches, and skills.

Ildi Arlette, CEO of Results Continuum in Calgary, Canada, described how she developed a growth mindset after having a fixed mindset for most of her life:

> I had absolutely no idea what growth mindset was until probably five years ago, and it's been one of the biggest eye-openers. I think, as a leader, you arrive with an air of knowing. That led to what I now know was the opposite of growth mindset. My biggest regret as a leader is I did not allow space for my clients, my

team, or even myself to truly develop because I had a very limited mindset. Learning what growth mindset is has completely redone my business.

I learned growth mindset when I decided to hire a coach, and our relationship developed in a very nontraditional way. One of the things I found with so many women leaders is that lots of us consider ourselves uncoachable. So what was interesting is I came to know this person because I was speaking at an E-Women Network event in Canada. She was the speaker after me. I never stay for the next speaker. But for some reason, I stayed and listened to her, and her message was around the thoughts in our mind and the stories we tell ourselves that are limiting us, stories that make us climb ladders up against someone else's wall, not our own. And even when we realize that, we don't seem to give ourselves permission to pick up the ladder and move it. So you end up constructing a life and a business and goals around external approval around the stories you've built. And it fascinated me because I consider myself a strong storyteller, and it made me look at my own stories and where they were leading and what they were keeping me from, which opened up a growth mindset for me.

Jennifer Peek, CEO of Peek Advisory Group in Kansas City, also learned about developing a growth mindset later in her career. She told me,

When I was in public accounting, every year, we had to get forty hours of CPE to maintain our license. Our firm sent us to training, and we had a guy who did a presentation on *Think and Grow Rich*, the book. So I got introduced to that sort of growth mindset early on, and receiving that book truly was one of the greatest gifts. It really makes you start thinking in a different way. And I think once you're open to concepts and ideas like that, your reticular activating system gets keyed, and then you start seeing things like Tony Robbins or *The 4-Hour Workweek*.

With a growth mindset, you can start to see those things and pick and choose what makes sense for you. I know that there are a lot of slams against *The 4-Hour Workweek* because you can't just work four hours a week. But there's some really good stuff in there that you can start doing. Just how have you applied that to the people that you lead in your business? What we really look at, from a growth mindset overall, regardless of what the source of the information is, is how do we not make this hard? Because there's more opportunities to make things hard than there are to make things easy.

I think when you have a growth mindset, you're always interested in what the next iteration of this looks like. And I think also it opens you up to the willingness to sow the seeds of change.

Lisa Hickey, a John Maxwell–certified leadership coach in Orlando, FL, talked about the importance of always being open to learning new things:

Being a perpetual learner, always actively being a student, to me, is probably the single thing that leads to everything else you can do because, if you're not learning, you're dying. Or, at the very least, stagnating. So I think that's pretty important. I don't think there's ever such a thing as, "I've completed my journey." There's always something new to learn. I feel the same way about people who don't like travel. I'm saying, how can you be a citizen of the world when you don't travel? Same thing about books. I don't understand people who don't like books. If you're not constantly learning, you'll be left behind. Above all the other things I've been taught and that I've learned, it would be to continue to have a passion for learning. There are so many people out there with so much to say. I just don't get not wanting to know that.

Penny Benkeser, the owner of nine Servpro franchises and a construction company in North Carolina, had a lot to say about being a perpetual learner and having a growth mindset, and how it's benefitted her since childhood:

> I think my love of learning started a long time ago with my parents. I grew up in a very blue-collar family. We didn't have a lot of money, but I started reading at a very early age, and so my parents leaned on that very heavily, and anytime an issue would come up, they thought, "There must be a book for that," even though they weren't necessarily broadly or well-read. They knew that I liked to read. When I was in the fourth grade, I had a really tough time with mean kids and bullying. I went through this really rough patch, and my dad bought me the Dale Carnegie book *How to Win Friends and Influence People*. I read that, and it started me down a path of understanding that we have our own life experiences, but we're only so good. I realized that outside of my family, there are books I can read that can help me understand the world around me better than I'm going to be able to. I don't want to just go through the school of hard lumps. I want to learn from other people's mistakes and try to learn from the people who study this stuff.
>
> So from fourth grade on, whenever there was an issue, my parents gave me a book. That includes my entire sex education, which came from books called *Life Cycle*, which was a whole set of books. I read them cover to cover, all of them. My friends used to come

over and look at them because they had very specific pictures and diagrams and all the rest of it. But I think that just started me down the path of knowing I can learn and gain knowledge.

Penny related another story about when a growth mindset benefited her:

> After college, I moved with a boy to San Francisco and didn't have a job. I didn't know anyone. I ended up getting a job with the Ford Financial Services Group, working with some of the smartest people I have ever worked with. A lot of them were ex-Wall Streeters who moved out to San Francisco, and they were all planning on retiring at thirty-five, and they were so damn smart. I had never worked around people like that in my life. They used words that I had no idea what on earth they were talking about. So I kept a little book, and I would write down all the stuff, whether it was a word or a concept or their reference points. I didn't even know what they were talking about. Like, Occam's razor, what the hell is that? I didn't know. So I'm writing down concepts; I'm writing down words. I would go home at night and look up the words, and then I would find somebody that I could trust and not be embarrassed and ask about the concepts.

> I worked for the bank for a very long time, and the culture became quite toxic. And so I left and started my own business. I was searching out anything I could find about business ownership, from *The E-Myth Revisited* to other books, trying to read and go to conferences and learn about how you scale a business and the pitfalls and all of that. And I valued the continuous learning mindset, particularly as somebody who came from the corporate world and moved into entrepreneurship, learning as broadly and as robustly as I could.

Penny told me that even now, after a few decades in business, she still wants to learn new things and continue to grow.

I just signed up for a class from one of the NYU professors at Stern. He's doing a strategic sprint class. It's available online and starting at the end of May for two weeks. And I'm really excited about that. Again, anything I can do to continuously learn to expand my mind.

I think people often don't know what good looks like. If you're surrounding yourself with mediocre, then you just don't know what's any better. If I just grew up in Florence, South Carolina, and I'd never left, I wouldn't be this person. But you keep pushing yourself and pushing your boundaries, and you recognize, "Oh, wait a minute. That is a lot better. Okay. What is that? Why? How do they get there? How do they know that?" And you just keep learning and figuring things out. And that's been a lifelong quest. I think it makes you more aware. I think it makes me a better business owner, a better parent. I think it's just fundamental to life, having that growth mindset behind everything that I do.

When a leader has a growth mindset, their employees are more committed to their work because they feel they can grow, learn, and thrive within the organization. Growth mindset leaders encourage creativity, allow their people to experiment, try new ideas, and see failure as a learning opportunity. To encourage a growth mindset in your people, praise them for their efforts, not only for the results. Instead of telling someone how smart they are, tell them you appreciate how hard they work, how much they've learned, or how much they've improved.

Encourage your people to constantly learn new things, take classes and workshops, watch TED talks, and read books. Ask them what they want to learn and encourage them to pursue their goals. Last year I sent all of the people on my team a copy of *The Compound Effect* by Darren Hardy, and once everyone read it, we talked about how to apply it to our jobs and lives. If I see a webinar advertised on a topic that would be of interest to one of my team members, I urge them to sign up for it (and I pay for it). Just like you should always be learning and growing, you also need to help your people to always be learning and growing.

CHAPTER TAKEAWAYS

→ A person with a growth mindset understands that talent is not innate and skills can be learned and improved, while a person with a fixed mindset believes that people are born with certain talents and capabilities, which are fixed for life.

→ Leaders with a growth mindset are more effective because they are open to learning new information, approaches, and competencies, which allows them to adapt to changes in their business environment.

→ Employees in companies with growth mindset leaders are happier because they can be more innovative and creative.

→ To encourage a growth mindset in your people, praise them for their efforts, not only for their results. Instead of telling someone how smart they are, tell them you appreciate how hard they work, how much they've learned, or how much they've improved.

Chapter 8

DON'T TAKE IT PERSONALLY

HEAR CRITICISM, LEARN FROM IT,
AND DON'T HOLD A GRUDGE

"Take criticism seriously, but not personally. If there is truth or merit in the criticism, try to learn from it. Otherwise, let it roll right off you."

—HILLARY CLINTON

Kathy Wilson, a leadership coach and the President of Coach Kathy Wilson, said to me,

Let me tell you a story. When I was on the women's basketball coaching staff at Ole Miss, I worked with a guy who was a recruiting coordinator. He was just mean, horrible. So I would be horrible back. And I actually was going to quit because it was just such a toxic environment. My first year, we almost got into a physical altercation; that's how bad the relationship was. And I initiated it, I will admit, he caught me on a bad day. He said something that I thought was completely inappropriate in front of our girls, and I grabbed him by his lapels, and I was literally about to just haul off and punch them. It was so toxic that that's how I had responded.

I went home and told my mom I wanted to quit. And I was telling her all the things that he was saying and doing. And she said, "I understand that he's not a good person, or he hasn't treated you very well, but you don't sound like you were yourself either. And I wonder what if it would be different if you went back and you were the Kathy that I know." And so, even though I didn't want to go back, I'm also a high D on the DiSC,[10] so it sounded like a challenge to me. So I went back, and I was just myself; I was upbeat, and I didn't let anything that he did get to me. About four or five months in, he invited me to dinner at his house. I thought he was going to poison me.

He tells me his story about how he grew up. It was horrible. It was nothing I could have imagined about not feeling loved and being displaced and how hard he worked to get this job. I didn't have to work that hard to get my job. I was coaching travel basketball, and somebody was like, "Oh, she's a great coach." He had to work his way up twenty years to get his job at Ole Miss. And when I left and took the job at GW, he cried. To this day, I adore him. Nobody understands how I just have this adoration for him. They're like, "He was so mean to you." But I realized that it wasn't about me.

He still was a jerk to everybody else, but I could say, "No, don't do that, don't talk to the girls like that, you're the coach, you've got to find a better way." And he would listen.

What I learned is that when you don't take other people's stuff and make it personal, it allows you the space to show up as your best self. Don't try to change the environment; change yourself and watch the environment around you change. I clearly recognize that I can't make him change for everybody else. But because I changed, I certainly had that first ring of influence on that circle that was directly around me, which he was in. And that was a very different experience. So I have seen that not taking things personally and not holding a grudge works. So when I tell people that in organizations, when I go in and train and they're like, "But my boss is all this." And I just say, "Let me tell you a story."

So many women take things personally that are not personal, and changing your perspective will help you be a more effective leader. For example, a client cancels your contract. Stan tells you it's because your service sucks and the client doesn't like you anymore. What do you say? "Screw you, Stan!" It's just as likely something happened within the client's organization that has nothing to do with you. Maybe one of their customers canceled an order, and they no longer have the money to pay you. Maybe their board wants to go in a different direction, and your services aren't applicable anymore. Those situations aren't personal, they're business decisions, and if you treat them as such, you'll be able to move on more quickly and with less angst.

But what if the client cancels and tells you directly it's because your service sucks, and Stan was right? You should still try not to take it personally but, instead, see it as an opportunity to improve. Ask them for specific examples of what didn't meet their expectations, then take a realistic look at their criticism and use it to fix a problem that you weren't aware of or improve your service. Or maybe the problem was them, in which case you can dismiss it and walk away.

Tammy Dickerson, the CEO of The Baker Group, a Los Angeles event management company, agrees. She uses "secret shoppers" at her events to provide feedback on the guest experience. She explained,

I would secretly invite these people to our events to have a guest experience and then come back and give me feedback on that experience. Sometimes it was good and sometimes not, but it allowed me to learn what we're doing well and what we could do better at, and then how to improve that. So I've always really, really been big on feedback. Because I think that's the only way you can grow and expand. Being able to listen for the truth and being able to put aside the pain and the hurt and the little sting of the truth. Put that aside and look at what your end goal is and how that truth is going to help you get there.

Tammy also talked about the importance of separating business from personal, especially since her sister is one of her key managers. She said,

Having my sister work for me is an area where I have to separate the business and the personal. I have to be able to be open and honest—when we're doing employee evaluations, when we're doing feedback from clients, when we're doing overall training and evaluation. I have to be able to take that personal side out of it and hear from her how I am as a manager and my leadership skills and how I can improve and what she likes and dislikes. But I also have to be able to give her that same kind of feedback. She does not take it personally either. And that was one of the ground rules that we had when she came to work for me is that we can't allow this business relationship to affect our sisterhood. So if we aren't able to separate it, then this is not a good business decision for you to come to work for us. And we both took some time to think about it, and she came back and said, "I think we can do it." And we've been doing it for almost seven years. So that has been good. But I really think it begins with the spirit of just being open and honest. I think that if you have the ability as a leader and a business owner to trust the person who is giving you the feedback, trust that the feedback is coming from a good place and that they really have your best interests at heart, then I think that takes the sting away a little bit.

Lynda Bishop, Vice President of National Programs at the NAWBO Institute for Entrepreneurial Development and a licensed relationship therapist, explained that there are real biological differences between women and men when it comes to taking things personally:

> Because we're so relationship bound, a lot of times the aggression between women is so subtle, it's indirect, and so it's easy to misread each other. It's so much easier with men. I mean, they're just directly in your face, and this is what it is. And then they move on. But we have a hard time letting go.

> It's fascinating because there are biological brain differences that make it harder for us not to hold a grudge. There's a story in the book *In the Company of Women* by Dr. Susan Murphy about chimpanzees and how we're just one DNA strand away from them and their natural behavior. You can see it in human beings as well. We have the same types of group behaviors in relationships as chimpanzees. Their group dynamics are really, really similar to ours. You know, they aren't being taught by the media. They're just natural, but they still do the same things.

> The male chimpanzees have a very clear hierarchy, and the females have a very clear culture of collaboration. The females share things, and they share duties, and they share child-rearing, and they share resources, and they make sure that everybody has food. They gather those things, and they share them with everybody. But if

one of the females injures somebody else's child or takes more food than she should, then the entire group turns on her and kicks her out. She is not welcome back, and she has to go find a new band of monkeys to live with, and hopefully, they don't kill her because they're also very territorial creatures.

What's interesting is that the males fight with each other, too, but they're fighting for power. So they're fighting to be the alpha male. Once they fight and the alpha male role is defined, or the new guy gets put in his place, or the old guy beats the new guy, and it's like, "Okay, you're the winner," they all go back to what they were doing, and nobody holds a grudge. The females don't hold a grudge against the males, but they hold a grudge against the other females, and they won't let her back in. And there's a huge percentage difference. Only 16 percent of the males hold a grudge, but 82 percent of the females hold a grudge. And this happens in nature. And so it's just super interesting because their relationships with each other are super important, and that's what keeps them alive.

And with human women, our relationships are super important, and we need each other, and we still feel aggression, but we just do it differently, and if one of us hurts another one or hurts us or does something that we deem really the wrong thing to do, we have a hard time forgiving each other. We might let you back in a little bit, but not as far as you were. We don't go back to start.

I mean, Doris (a woman we both know who had behaved badly) could come to me today and say, "I'm so sorry for everything I did," and I'd be like, "Okay, I forgive you, but you're out. You were voted off that Island, and you're out. You're out, and you're not coming back. You have to find a new band of monkeys."

Another story in her book is that while the female chimpanzees will kick out a female for hurting another female, they will also band together and protect another female from an aggressive male. And so it works both ways. They protect each other, even from one of the males in the same group, but he's still an outsider because he's not a female. I mean, he's one that maybe every one of them has had sex with. But they don't have the same relationship with the males that they do with each other. And they will protect each other from an aggressive male inside their own group. But then when they chase him off, and he comes back later, and he's being nice, they'll take him back in. They don't hold a grudge against him, but they will against the female.

And this totally applies to women because we are harder on each other by far. So staying aware of things like that, I think it's really important to understand that and then be able to identify it in yourself. To make sure that I'm not harder on another female simply because they're female and they should know better. Because she's yanked my chain one too many times in the past, where if a guy had done it, I'd be like, "Yeah, he's just an ass," but I wouldn't worry about it.

So a good example of that is Peter (not his name) from the ABC program. He's an asshole. He's always an asshole. I know he's an asshole. I expect him to be one. I don't take it personally because I know that that's just the way he is. Because he's a guy, and I have lower expectations of men being able to be good at relationships. So my expectation of him is much, much, much, much, much lower than my smart and amazing relationship-equipped female friends who I know can do better. I don't think he can [do better], and so it doesn't need to be there that he would want to. And even if he wanted to, his brain just can't do it. Sometimes he tries.

I see him try, and he just doesn't understand how to do it. Those wires just don't cross. He doesn't get it, so he doesn't maliciously do things, and maybe that's the difference.

Maybe the difference is because I really don't believe that he does things maliciously because he's so straightforward. Whereas a woman, take Doris as an example, since I worked with both of them in the same project, I watched my back constantly because she wouldn't be straightforward with me. But if I felt a knife twisting in my back, I was pretty sure she was high on the list of people. I would look to see if it was her. And so she felt much more dangerous to me than Peter because Peter would just tell me straight out.

Jennifer Peek, CEO of Peek Advisory Group in Kansas City, agreed that men and women are different in this regard. She said,

I'm in a very male-dominated field, and I don't generally run into issues because of that. I've always gotten a level of respect, and that's a fortunate thing for me to be able to say. I think that there is a tough skin that you have to develop when you're dealing with men because they just communicate differently. I don't ever really feel like I'm being mansplained to or talked down to, but I can see it in the way that they talk in certain instances.

I think you have to be able to compartmentalize some of that stuff and be like, "They're not bad guys. They're not trying to be dicks, but they don't take things personally, and you have to learn not to also." And that is probably the biggest thing. They don't take things personally. It's really interesting to me because gender is not the issue here where they make it personal. I've had at least one client say, "I'm very disappointed in you," for something that I couldn't control, like I couldn't get their bank to approve a loan. I learned a lesson from that, and those are the types of clients we're not going to work with.

I think a lot of women get held back because they do take things personally that aren't necessarily even meant personally. I have a good friend who started out as more of a business connection that's become a good friend. We do not operate in the same space. She has never really been in corporate America. So if people don't pay her, that is like a personal attack, and it is always very personal with her. And I'm like, "It's not personal. Or even if it is, you can't take it that way." This is business, and your ability to react in a professional manner to assure that you get paid is going to be influenced by the fact that you're taking it personally. Now you've attached all this emotion to it. And it could just be that they didn't get a payment from one of their customers and so they couldn't pay on time. It could have nothing to do with you. So I asked her, "What is your collection process like? You need a collection process like send a follow-up email at fifteen days or thirty days, or a letter at ninety days." I had a conversation with her where she said, "I did this presentation on Friday, and I sent the invoice out that afternoon, and I still haven't gotten paid." It was Monday. I'm serious. I said, "Like three days ago you did this, and it was not a lot of money. It was less than five hundred dollars. Oh my goodness." And her question to me was, "What should I do? How should I follow up?" I told her that she's gotta toughen it up a little bit. I think that if you have a company and you need somebody to do collections, you need to find somebody who's not attached to collecting the money, who is focused on doing a good job.

I think, especially as leaders, women definitely take things way too personally at times. That's something that in order to be a more effective leader, you really have to get past. With a lot of our clients, we know things about their companies and the financials that nobody else in their company knows. So we end up both as sounding boards and therapists and sometimes get the brunt of their frustration. It's important to be able to not get emotionally involved, otherwise you can't do your job well. You can't be a good leader if you can't. You can have empathy and sympathy and all of those things that I think make women really good leaders. And you have to know where that line stops.

What if one of your coworkers or your boss is regularly nasty to you? Again, look at the situation, and determine what's really going on. Is that person nasty to everyone or just to you? Is it the person's issue, or is it the corporate culture? Some companies foster such a competitive environment that some people see their coworkers as people to beat, not people to work with.

When I was at Arthur Andersen, they had a very rigid hierarchical structure and a policy of "up or out," which meant that every year you had to be ready to be promoted to the next level or you were let go. As a result, some people got very competitive, especially with the others at their level. They didn't realize that making their team as a whole look good made them look even better; they thought they had to stand out alone and tried to do that by tearing other people down. Turns out, the ones who focused on cultivating strong working relationships with their team members ended up being the most successful and got promoted every year.

Some companies have such a toxic environment or are so understaffed that everyone is perennially stressed out, either by the unprofessional atmosphere or the unreasonable amount of work they are expected to do. In those situations, again, realize that when people behave toward you in unprofessional ways, it's not necessarily personal.

What if you assess the situation, the person's actions, and the corporate culture and determine that it really is personal? Someone just really doesn't like you. Maybe they don't like you because you got the promotion they wanted. Or because you shut down their idea in a meeting. Or because you wore the same blouse as them and looked better in it. Or the boss likes you better, and they're jealous.

Even if it is personal, try not to take it personally. Accept that not everyone is going to like you, and move on. I'm not saying this is easy because it's not. It can hurt when people criticize your company, your services, your products, or you as an individual. I'm also not saying you should put up with a situation where there's bullying, harassment, or discrimination because you absolutely shouldn't. In those cases, you need to report it and/or remove yourself from the situation.

In her MasterClass, Anna Wintour, the longtime editor of *Vogue* magazine, said,

> It's very important to remember that not everybody is going to always agree with you and that you will be, at times in your career, criticized, maybe strongly, maybe in ways that might hurt you. You shouldn't ignore it; you can't pretend it's not happening. I think it's very helpful, actually, to listen to criticism, to hear what people have to say; you can often learn from it. But at the same time, you have to remain true to your own vision...there will be those who disagree, but you can't be everything to everybody, and you have to accept that and plant your flag in the ground in the way you feel is most appropriate to the route that you're taking.

Similar to the mindset of mastering your inner voice (see Chapter 1), not taking things personally is an internal mindset that only *you* can control. By looking internally and connecting with yourself, you can face this challenge head-on and overcome it. Maybe not every time, in every circumstance, but as long as you're improving, you're leveling up your leadership skills.

Penny Benkeser, the owner of nine Servpro franchises and a construction company in North Carolina, agrees. She told me,

> My dad was a manager of a trucking terminal, and one thing he taught me a long time ago was there's no crying in corporate America. He was a very good manager and cared very deeply about his people. But there's no crying at work. If you've got a problem or an issue, call me. They don't take it personally, and if you do take it personally, then call me and let's talk about it. But you've got to learn to toughen up.
>
> He always said that I had the thinnest skin of anybody that he ever knew. And that's true. I do. I have extremely thin skin, and I struggle mightily not to take things personally or to not let people know that I take them personally. Many times I can recognize the difference in how it makes me feel versus how I should react to it.
>
> But you learn that in a corporate setting, in the conference rooms, you can't show emotion. You have to be very objective because nobody wants to hear your personal crap. It's about business. It's about the thing. And the more that you can do that and the more that you can be objective, I think that helps you make decisions better.
>
> One of the things that brought this home was being the presi-

dent of the NAWBO Charlotte Board. I was newer to business ownership when I was the president. I think I'd been in business for like three years. And I said, "We're going to run this like a business. NAWBO is a business. Our chapter is a business. We're going to run it like that." And so in our meetings, I said, "We're going to use our meetings for decision-making. We're going to put the information out there ahead of time to have a chance to weigh in on your opinions, then in the meeting, we're gonna make the decision."

But I sat on the NAWBO Board, and time after time, I'd watch women start to cry. I'd watch them get up and go to the bathroom. The women get so butt-hurt because they would bring something to the table, and it was because their idea was not accepted. One of them even came back after meeting and said, "Y'all are being mean to me." I'm like, "Where do you get that?" "You didn't choose my idea." And it's like, "Yeah, but we didn't choose her idea or her idea. We chose this idea. You know, we voted on that." Over and over again, they would take it personally, and it's so hard in a setting like that to say, "Can everybody just put your big girl panties on and get over yourself? This is about business." We'll let the best idea win, whoever's that is, and if it's mine or not mine, I don't care. We're trying to solve this as an organization, but it is really particularly hard for women. That might be my bias just because I've been around so many men in the workplace, but it seems like it's harder for women. But I find it as critical to decision-making, to running boards or being on a board, to running your business, to whatever it is. You know, it helps you make clearer, better decisions if you can extract the personal from it. And it's easy to say and hard to do, granted.

I've often thought about where it stems from. I grew up with a brother, and he and I grew up ribbing each other, and I can give it hard, but I'll also take it. And my dad used to say that you've got to learn to get as good as you give. You can't just give it and not take it. But you know, if you watch men when they grow up with brothers, they razz each other all the time; they call each other and say, "Oh, nice shirt, did you get that at Home Depot?" Men don't care. But women never do that. And so I think that men learned that thicker skin, that razzing, that give and take. I think that's their culture. Women are so affirmative to each other, "Oh, you look so pretty."

My daughters, when they come downstairs, I'll say, "Nice zit," and it's not bad; I'm just trying to teach them how to have a thicker skin and not take themselves so damn seriously. Anyway, I wonder if that's the root of it in the way that men do not take it personally because they razz each other endlessly. But we women don't do that. We really don't do that.

I think during my years in corporate, I developed a shell. You have to draw on that armor that you go into work with every day. And I still bring that into my business today, and I think it makes me a better business owner. I think it makes me a better manager of our people, a leader of our people.

Kathy Wilson told me that she does a lot of mediating between people who have taken things personally. She tells them that they have to understand that what other people do is not about them. She says,

What you do is not about me. What you do is about you. I always say, assume good intent. That's my biggest thing. I assume good intent. I don't care what has happened. I want you to assume good intent and then go from there.

And then, let's look at why we are in this conflict and see what the root of this conflict really is so that we can alleviate it. But you can only ever get there if you don't take things personally in the first place. I always say, don't put other people's stuff in your purse and then carry it around. Close your purse, stop taking other people's stuff, putting it in there, and then carrying it around and making it about you. You need to be able to hear criticism and learn from it, and don't hold a grudge. What is the saying? It's like taking poison and hoping the other person will die. It's so useless and energy-consuming, whereas that energy could be put into other places.

Instead of criticism, I always say feedback. You have to separate how something is said, which is hard. Because I know the other side of it, I'm a big communicator, but you don't get to dictate how everybody else communicates. So you have to listen to what's being said, versus how it's being said, and assume good intent. And take away those things that are really going to help you grow.

Relationships are nothing but a mirror. Every relationship that you're in, whether it's a friendship or romantic relationship or a work relationship, it's a mirror. And it's there to help you to grow into the best version of yourself or the best leader you can be. You have one of two ways of reacting to feedback or criticism. You can say, "Oh my God, why are you saying that to me? I can't believe you're saying that to me. I can't believe you do not see how hard I'm working." Or you can say, "Hm, what is this moment trying to show me. Whether it's the feedback that I'm getting or how I'm responding to it, what am I supposed to be learning in this moment that is going to make me a better leader?"

So when that feedback comes, if you're triggered by it, that means you've got two learning experiences there. What is the feedback, and what is the feedback telling me that maybe I need to work on? Why am I so triggered by this, and what is that trying to show me?

So unless you are at the point where you've actually physically assaulted somebody, there's hope for you because there was hope for me. And I was so embarrassed by my Ole Miss story for years because it was so out of character for me. But now I recognize why it happened because it was something that I was supposed to share with other people to help them understand that there is power in showing up as your highest self and not taking things personally and making them about you and drowning in that grudge, holding resentment and that toxicity that can occur when you think everybody's against you.

The fact is that they're not; it's just that story you're spinning in your head where you are the center of the universe, and everything is about you. They're worried about their stuff. So if you worried about your stuff, then you would be able to ascend. Or at least have the energy to take on the things in the organization that's real versus the stuff that you're making up.

CHAPTER TAKEAWAYS

→ In order to be an effective leader, you need to learn not to take things personally and not to hold a grudge.

→ When you find yourself holding a grudge against another woman, consider if you would let her off the hook if a man had done or said the same thing.

→ In the event of conflict, review the situation and determine if other factors could have caused the other person to say/act as they did that have nothing to do with you.

→ Always assume good intent on the other person's part.

PART 2

CONNECTING WITH OTHERS

Chapter 9

EMBODY SERVANT LEADERSHIP

LEADERSHIP ISN'T ABOUT THE LEADER

"Leadership should be born out of the understanding of the needs of those who would be affected by it."

—MARIAN ANDERSON

All of the previous chapters have been about different aspects of leadership that are internal; how you think and develop a leadership mindset. This chapter and the ones that follow are about how you connect with the people you are leading because you can't influence those who don't feel connected to you. For people to feel connected to you, they need to feel like they know the real you, not just the façade that you portray, and can identify with you—warts and all. They also need to feel like you know them, understand them, and understand how they feel.

Servant leadership is the mindset of understanding that the leader's most important role is to serve the people and organization that she leads. I was first introduced to the concept of servant leadership in NAWBO. As I've previously said, one of the things that got me interested in leadership was my experience serving in leadership positions within NAWBO, first in my local chapter, then at the national level. When I first got involved, one of NAWBO's biggest challenges was that chapter leadership turned over every year, and each year, a new president would come in wanting to start from scratch and implement their own programs and ideas. Basically, many people wanted to be chapter presidents for their own personal reasons—to promote their businesses and themselves, not necessarily to help the organization or the other members.

When Jen Earle, the current NAWBO National CEO, took over, she instituted a culture of servant leadership to refocus the chapter leaders and members on the nature of those positions—to benefit the organization and its members, not just the individuals in those positions. She instituted long-term strategic plans at the national level so that individual leaders would focus on achieving the previously established goals versus derailing the progress made in preceding years. She also established a program to incentivize chapters to do the same.

Jen explained it to me:

> I think that the servant leadership thing was because, too often, I saw people stepping up in their own right, wanting to make their own legacy, and it was really difficult for them to see what was happening around them. You have other people that are the same caliber of leader try to conform to one person standing and saying, "It is going to be my way this time." So that's why I adopted it for the organization because I felt like it was important to say, "Look, it's not about you. It can't be about you," especially in NAWBO.
>
> When someone comes in to lead in a way of no flexibility and not

connecting the person to the job and not connecting their needs as a person, then you have all sorts of terrible things that happen. I felt like they were trying to build an empire, and that's really amazing, but they're doing it at the expense of humanity, and humanity, I think, is the biggest deal. And I think that's one thing that's just prevalent across the country, maybe even around the world, that there's the lack of human connection. It's more connected to the technology than to the heart. I think that's where the biggest fail is.

Being a leader with our team, I put myself in the position of each person I work with and with the board, and I think, *How are they going to feel about this outcome? How are they going to feel about this approach? How's it going to impact them?* So when they're reading this information or they're hearing this information, what is that going to look like for them? Is it going to be striking a nerve, or is it going to be touching their heart? Are they gonna feel like they're empowered? Are they going to feel discouraged?* I just know that I want to make sure that whoever I'm working with, whether my team, whether my board, whether it's a member, that I connect with them on a human level and that the human connection is very, very important.

Darla Beggs, CEO of ABBA Staffing in Dallas, TX, and a past NAWBO National Board Chair agrees:

I think I learned to be a better business leader and a servant leader in NAWBO because, in that organization, you're dealing with everyone as a volunteer. You really can't tell anybody what to do. You have to work through it and get them to buy in, to listen to what they have to say about it to see if there's some modification that needs to be made, to get along with everyone. That's what we know about all the boards I served on.

And there were highly different opinions about things on some of those boards, but I always said, "Lead from the middle. You can't be on one side or another." You've got to let all of it come together and then try to sort through the democracy of leading everybody along and getting everyone's consensus—even though there might not be total buy-in. So I think learning to do that or practicing doing that on a regular basis probably made me a better leader at work because, again, instead of telling people what to do, I encourage them to tell me what they need or what they want or how they feel their job could be better. I think that had I not gone through that whole process of learning to be a servant leader within NAWBO, I'm not sure my business would be as successful as it is.

Jeanette Armbrust, Managing Director of Skyline Exhibits of Greater Los Angeles, CA, and another NAWBO past National Board Chair, agreed with Darla that learning about servant leadership through her NAWBO service changed the way she ran her company. She told me,

When I first started the company, I remember being like, "This is my company. I get to make all the decisions. I'm in charge, and this is how we're going to do it," because I didn't know any better. And so, I think I evolved more into servant leadership and just realizing that you get more flies with honey than with vinegar. But when I got on the NAWBO Board, that really changed my mindset and made me realize, *This isn't about you. If you really want to be successful, Jeanette, it can't be the Jeanette show. It has to be a collaboration.*

And that's when I started to really look into leadership and realized that on the Board, people didn't have to do what I said. It was not my deal. I'm one vote. So that really helped to shape the leader that I became in my business and really changed my whole mentality into being more of a servant leader. I learned that when you reach out and serve the people, not only your customers but your team in general, that it helps all ships rise.

I noticed that when I had more of that mindset that I was more successful, and my company was more successful. My team members noticed that change. I used to meet every Tuesday afternoon at one o'clock with all the department managers. And we would go through our agenda and get an update on what was going on. And at one meeting, I remember them actually saying, "We have noticed that you changed your leadership style and that you are much more collaborative than you used to be."

I changed into more asking than telling, more "What do you think about that? What do you think we should do? How do you think we should run that?" And then also I got a business coach, which was really helpful for me to learn how to become a better leader and really a servant leader and realized that my job as a leader is to build others up and to serve other people. And it's not about raising myself but raising everybody else.

Traditional organizations believe that their focus should be on maximizing shareholder returns, which leads to more money for the company, which leads to better products/services, which leads to paying employees more, which theoretically leads to happy employees. Conversely, companies with a servant leadership culture believe that their focus should be on engaging employees and satisfying customers, ultimately delivering value to all stakeholders.

In traditional leadership doctrine, the leader is the boss, and everyone else is there to do as the boss orders. In servant leadership, the leader is there to connect with and serve those she is leading: the organization as a whole, its employees, its customers, and other stakeholders. Traditional organizations show their organizational structure as a pyramid, with the leadership on top and employees on the bottom. Organizations with a servant leadership culture often show their organization chart as an upside-down pyramid, with the employees on top and leadership on the bottom to reflect that it's the leaders who are supporting the employees.

Studies have shown that two-thirds of workers feel underappreciated, and half of those are searching for new jobs at any given time. Organizations with a culture of servant leadership generally have a higher level of employee satisfaction and engagement than traditional organizations, which leads to higher productivity, higher morale, lower absenteeism, lower turnover, and higher profits.

You often see a servant leadership culture in nonprofit organizations, but it can benefit all organizations. Servant leadership is a mindset shift from the standard authoritarian leadership style found in traditional corporations. Servant leaders believe in the power of teamwork, while authoritarian leaders believe the team is there to do what they say. Servant leaders share the credit for success, while authoritarian leaders keep it for themselves.

Organizations with a culture of servant leadership succeed because employees feel empowered and inspired by a purpose larger than themselves. For example, someone in the accounting department in a traditional organization might think of their job as running the numbers to help maximize shareholder profit. That's not very inspiring, especially if they aren't a shareholder. But if they see their job as making sure the company has the necessary resources to make products that will help a mother take care of her newborn baby, they will be more invested in doing a good job and feel like they're contributing to the greater good.

Maria Gamb, Founder of NMS Communications and author of *Values-Based Leadership for Dummies,* told me,

> For me, servant leadership is never about me. It's always about teaching everybody to do the right thing, to be the best they can, and to always think of the person next to them. And I always thank my father, who was a New York City detective, because he actually taught me this lesson really young. I'm one of four kids, and if one of us got in trouble, we all got in trouble. We're a unit, and we take care of each other. I mean, it's such a cop mentality, but it really does work when you are in the workforce. You have to have each other to rely on.
>
> I always tell people that you have to remember why you're here. You have to remember why what you're doing is important. I struggled with this myself for many years. I was sitting around with some of my team members, and I asked them, "Why are you here?"
>
> And they're like, "The money is good." I'm like, "Okay, but why do you do what you do? Because you want to be creative, but what is your creativity bringing into the world?" And then we all thought about the fact that we actually provide the clothing for people to go and find jobs, to celebrate important events in life, and understand that it doesn't matter what you do as long as you understand that you're benefiting the greater good of people, and it changed everybody's perception, especially when they were feeling very down, to think about how we serve others.

A servant leader is focused not on what is best for herself but on what is best for the organization as a whole, and she sees her role as helping to achieve that. She sees her job as helping her employees be the best they can be, cultivating a culture of trust and collaboration, and fostering innovation and creativity. She also wants to make sure that the organization is serving its customers to the maximum extent possible by providing the goods and/or services that the customers need in the most beneficial way.

Thresette Briggs, CEO of Performance 3 LLC in Indianapolis, IN, told me that she didn't learn about servant leadership until she left her corporate job and got her master's degree. She said,

> I was always shown in corporate America that leadership was supposed to be "You gotta do this, you gotta do that." And I always had this feeling where it was about other people, but it was presented to me as something else. I started learning more about servant leadership when I was getting my master's degree. I realized it wasn't about me. Yes, I am a person with a title and the person that's supposed to support people and make sure that they have what they need, but I'm not supposed to treat people the way I had been treated. In the corporate world, it was not a collaborative relationship. It was not a "listening to them" relationship; it was more of an authoritarian type of a leadership role. And that never really agreed with me.

> So once I got more into leadership, I realized it's more about being collaborative, letting people tell you what they need, and then helping them get it because they will be a lot more effective for them and for you if you use a servant leadership approach. I began to do that.

> I decided to get out of corporate America because I felt I was

not getting a balance in my personal, professional, and spiritual life, which was very important to me. So when I developed my business model, I wanted it to be one that incorporated my spiritual gifts, as well as my professional strengths. That would allow me to more effectively be a better servant leader. So it was more about doing what I was called to do in the way I was called to do it.

In my past corporate jobs, I had all kinds of leaders. I had a leader who would beat on his desk and yell at his team, and that never went over well with me. I have a "three strikes, you're out" type of rule. And he did the third time, and I said, "You know what? My dad didn't yell at me, and my husband doesn't yell at me, so you will not yell at me." I could've lost my job that day. But he looked at me and said, "I didn't think I was yelling." I said, "Yeah, you're yelling." He said, "No, I'm just elevating my voice."

So, I had those kinds of leaders, but I also had the opposite kind of leader. I had those who were the servant leaders. And again, a lot of this I experienced before I actually learned about what servant leadership was. And then I learned about it, I understood, this is what it is. And I can distinguish the difference, and I can determine what kind of leader I want to be, based on learning this new lens that I have, and it helps me to see myself in this light. So it was a really good experience.

One common misconception about servant leadership is that servant leaders are so focused on making their employees successful that they do their jobs for them or let them off the hook for poor performance. In reality, this is not what serving their employees means. While effective servant leaders focus on helping their employees be successful, they need to be careful not to cater to their employees but to hold them accountable while ensuring they have the resources and autonomy to do their jobs.

Effective servant leaders need to remember that while their focus is on making their employees successful, they cannot abdicate their responsibility to the organization as a whole. They are still the leader and need to make sure the organization's goals and objectives are being met and, if not, institute corrective action. They should first ask themselves if they could have better supported their people in achieving their goals. But if an employee is not getting the job done, even after getting the resources and training needed, the leader needs to let them go.

Servant leaders also need to make the hard decisions in times of difficulty or crisis. A benefit of servant leadership is that when a difficult situation occurs and a tough decision needs to be made, the leader has usually earned enough trust and goodwill from the employees that they will accept the decision.

Tammy Dickerson, CEO of The Baker Group, an event management company in Los Angeles, shared her perspective:

> I tell everybody that we're a team, and that's why it's called The Baker Group because I do not do this alone. As you know, as the business owner, most people see our face, they see our name, and they want to recognize us, but it is not about me. It is clearly the team and the support system and the family of us working together that makes it successful. I feel like we work together as a team, and it's important. I never really got hung up on that until my sister Carlotta came to work for me. And then some people thought that she was the owner because her last name is Baker.

That brings up a story. Years ago, we were setting up a ballroom for an event, and we were running a little behind. I told the team that everybody's got to jump in and help. And I was setting the tables, and the manager of the hotel came in and said, "I need to talk to the owner of the company," and my associates said, "She is at one of the tables." And he says, "Oh, no, not her, I mean, the owner of The Baker Group." He couldn't believe that the owner was setting the table. It was just another example of being in the trenches with your troops and being able to show them that I will do anything that I'm asking you to do. It's a team effort, and I respect your work as much as I hope you respect mine as the CEO. It's been really powerful to have a group of people who've been with me as long as they have. And I think it's because I want to see them grow and expand, inspire, and continue to be fruitful.

CHAPTER TAKEAWAYS

→ Servant leadership is about understanding that being a leader is not about promoting or elevating yourself but about serving and elevating the people and organization you lead.

→ Traditional leadership principles are authoritarian and hierarchical, while servant leadership inverts the traditional organizational pyramid.

→ Servant leaders believe in the power of teamwork, while authoritarian leaders believe the team is there to do what they say.

→ Servant leaders share the credit for success, while authoritarian leaders keep it for themselves.

→ Servant leadership is giving your employees the tools and training to do their jobs and then letting them succeed and be recognized.

Chapter 10

DEMONSTRATE EMPATHY

UNDERSTAND WHERE OTHERS ARE COMING FROM

"The struggle of my life created empathy—I could relate to pain, being abandoned, having people not love me."

—OPRAH WINFREY

The last two years I worked at Arthur Andersen, I led the proposal team, which was arranged unusually: junior consultants, two at a time, did a four-month rotation with me to work on proposals for new business. This gave them an understanding of the marketing and business development process that most consultants at their level did not have. Being on my team often accelerated the careers of these individuals since it gave them more exposure to the senior managers and partners in the office than a typical junior consultant would have, and with it, the opportunity to make a good impression.

One day, one of my team members, whom I'll call Mary, a young woman who was only a year or two out of college, came to me and told me that one of the (female) managers had commented to her that her attire was unprofessional because her pants were too tight. Mary was really upset and asked if she should go home and change. I remembered the early days of my own career, when I was always worried if I was dressed professionally, and how mortified I had been when someone once commented on my skirt being too short. I told her that I understood how she felt, then I went to the manager who had made the comment, had a conversation with her about the insensitivity of her comment, and asked her to apologize to Mary, which she did.

I'll be honest, this happened over twenty years ago, and I had completely forgotten about it until Mary recently reminded me about it. She wrote a post on LinkedIn about the incident, thanking me for being empathetic and a role model in her career.

One of the best ways to connect with others is through empathy. Empathy means having the ability to understand the needs of others, being aware of their feelings and thoughts, and seeing a situation from their point of view. Leaders who demonstrate empathy create an environment of open communication, collaboration, and innovation. Oprah Winfrey once stated that "leadership is about empathy. It is about having the ability to relate to and connect with people for the purpose of inspiring and empowering their lives."

Sheryl Sandberg, the COO of Facebook, got a lot of public criticism for lacking empathy after her book *Lean In* was published. In the book, she talked about the need for women to be more assertive in the workplace, raise their hands and take their rightful seat at the conference room table. While that was all great, she didn't show an understanding that many women have different life circumstances that didn't allow them to "lean in" as she was instructing, such as single mothers. After her husband died suddenly in 2015, that changed, and she acknowledged that, "I think I got this all wrong before; I tried to assure people that it would be okay, thinking that hope was the most comforting thing I could offer. Real empathy is sometimes not insisting that it will be okay but acknowledging that it is not."

Expressing empathy is not a weakness; it's another way of connecting with other people, as we discussed in the chapters on authenticity and approachability. Empathy is not the same as sympathy; sympathy means understanding someone else's suffering but not necessarily feeling it. On the other hand, empathy means actually experiencing someone else's feelings and emotions. Even if you haven't experienced exactly what the other person is going through, you can demonstrate empathy by imagining yourself in the situation and understanding what it would feel like. Expressing empathy is also demonstrating vulnerability because you have to connect with your own emotions to identify with the other person's feelings.

In her TEDx talk, professor and author Brené Brown states, "Empathy drives connection, while sympathy drives disconnection." She defines four qualities of empathy: the ability to recognize the perspective of another person, not judging the other person, recognizing the other person's emotion, and communicating that recognition. Brown also says, "Rarely can a response make something better. What makes something better is connection."

Jen Earle, CEO of NAWBO, told me,

> One of the things I loved about Brené Brown's latest book, *Dare to Lead*, was about the tie of empathy and the importance of vulnerability and being a real person, especially in a time where it's so easy to not be, with technology and all of that.

There are many leaders that aren't empathetic. And so, I think about what does leadership look like outside of not being empathetic? Is there a way to be a really good leader and not have empathy? Is that a possibility? I don't know. And is there a correlation between the men in these situations, and do they have empathy?

As a leader, it's important to understand how to respond with empathy when someone comes to you with a problem. If the problem is work-related, something that's fixable, and they're looking for a solution, they most likely want your help in resolving the issue. However, if the problem is personal and/or not fixable, that is when you need to respond with empathy. Two ways to damage the connection are to try to solve their problem when they don't want your help or to try to find a silver lining. For example, if someone tells you that they're stressed because their child is struggling in school, don't recommend a tutor unless they ask if you know someone. Also, don't say something like, "At least your kid is getting C's; he could have failed out." Instead, think about how you would feel if it was your kid struggling, express how difficult it must be, and ask how they're handling it and what kind of support they need.

Lynda Bishop, the Vice President of National Programs at the NAWBO Institute for Entrepreneurial Development, agrees:

> Empathy is so important, getting out of your own head. You've got to get out of your own head and understand what somebody else's perspective is, what are they going through, and how does this really affect them, and you have to care about that. I find it really satisfying and fulfilling because you get to take yourself out of it, and so it makes room for you to actually care about other people.

Being empathetic is a basis for building trust among your team, which leads to higher engagement and productivity. When people feel appreciated and understood, they feel more connected to the organization and to you as the leader, and they tend to be more engaged and work harder. On the other hand, disengaged employees stop caring about their work, get less done, are more prone to mistakes, and are less likely to stay with your organization.

Jacinda Ardern, the Prime Minister of New Zealand, recently stated, "One of the criticisms I've faced over the years is that I'm not aggressive enough or assertive enough or maybe somehow, because I'm empathetic, it means I'm weak. I totally rebel against that. I refuse to believe that you cannot be both compassionate and strong."

CHAPTER TAKEAWAYS

→ Empathy is about seeing things from the perspective of others, not just feeling sorry for someone but understanding how they feel.

→ Empathy is putting yourself in another's shoes. Not only do they appreciate your effort, but you are also better able to understand what they need to make a stronger contribution to your organization.

→ Having empathy for your team members builds trust when they know you understand their perspective.

Chapter 11

SHOW AUTHENTICITY

BE AND SHOW WHO YOU GENUINELY ARE, WARTS AND ALL

"You have to remember the value of your individuality, that you have something different to offer that nobody else can."

—JENNIFER LOPEZ

Growing up in the eighties, I was always told that the most important attribute to be successful was professionalism. You always had to be calm, cool, and collected, and never show emotion. So when I got my first job and went out into the business world, that's how I tried to be. I am generally pretty even-keeled anyway, but at work, I would try to be serious all the time. I made friends at my jobs, and we had fun together outside the office, but I kept it professional during business hours.

A few years after starting our business, Diana told me that some of our employees were nervous around me. I was shocked. I had always treated our employees professionally, but because of that, they found me to be scary.

One of our employees once told me that she didn't want to tell me about a mistake she had made because she was afraid I would yell at her. I asked her, "Have I ever yelled at you?" and she replied, "No." I then asked, "Have you ever heard me yell at anyone?" She again responded that she hadn't. I wanted to know, "Then why did you think I would yell at you today?" She answered that even though I had never yelled at anyone, I often seemed like I was on the brink of yelling at someone.

That was eye-opening. After that conversation, I made a concerted effort to be less serious at the office, to crack jokes in staff meetings, and to show more of my authentic self and personality. In my daily huddles with my team, I regularly tell them about my screw-ups or when things haven't gone according to plan. I'm not perfect, and I don't want them to expect perfection from me, nor do I want them to think I expect perfection from them. As a result, I feel more connected to my team because I'm willing to share more of myself with them, including when things aren't going well, and I'm struggling, and they're willing to share the same with me.

Remember, you can't influence people who don't feel connected to you. If you are not authentic as a person and a leader, how on earth can people connect with you? They can't, of course. Do you feel connected to celebrities and politicians you don't know personally? It's unlikely that you do because we don't see an authentic version of them. We see their avatar, the person they project into the world, not their authentic selves. As a leader, you can choose to be real or project an idealized version of yourself. People will admire and connect with the former, not the latter.

Jessica Billingsley, CEO of Akerna in Denver, CO, agrees. She said,

I have found that as a leader, at the end of the day, if you're leading, you still have to make decisions. You have to be decisive; you have to lead. And in order to do that, there is an amount of bossiness or an amount of assertiveness that is just necessary. And what I think is helpful, from a standpoint of authenticity, is if you are making decisions, being able to share and to be vulnerable.

For example, I was just visiting with one of the companies that we're acquiring, and in every area where I could feel I was starting to dig in and they were getting a little defensive, I made an effort to share something like, here's how we've screwed it up in the past, and here's one of the things that we've found works and just being able to be very honest, very vulnerable and admit, we don't get it right all the time, but here's some things we've learned along the way.

When I am giving someone on my team feedback, I try very hard to share that I messed this up, or here's an example of a time where I missed something like this, and here's what I did to rise from that. And being willing to share that kind of thing, it goes a very, very long way, I have found.

When you think about the leaders who you really admire, what do you think about? Their accomplishments, sure, but also their struggles and how they overcame them. When people achieve things easily, without hard work and struggle, others admire their accomplishments but don't feel connected to them. We connect with someone by seeing the whole person they are: their true personality, what they really care about, their strengths and weaknesses, and their triumphs and failures. So your people can't connect with you unless you let them see the whole you.

Thresette Briggs, CEO of Performance 3 LLC in Indianapolis, told me that she used to be embarrassed about growing up in Wichita, Kansas. She said,

> I thought that I wasn't good enough because that's where I was from. That was subconscious. I didn't really think I felt that way, but I realized I did. So, later on, I began to understand that if I'm going to really be effective, if I'm going to be a leader and help others, then I have to embrace who I am—where I'm from—and own that. So I began to appreciate who I am and where I'm from and use them as strengths.

> Yes, I'm from Wichita. Yes, my name is Thresette. You know, there's an interesting story behind that, too, because I don't really feel like I embraced myself fully because of it. Thresette has been my name my whole life, of course. But when you're young and your name is unusual, and you're trying to help people learn how to pronounce your name with the spelling, and they're mispronouncing it. And you've been raised not to talk back to adults, not to debate. Then you just don't say anything, and they mispronounce your name. So after a while, I just said, "Call me Kay," which is my middle name.

> I used Kay until 2010 because I was making it easier for everybody else. But when I started my business, I wanted to be bold. I wanted to be courageous. I wanted to do things. So I did two things. I did zip lining because I had to get over my fear of heights. And I took my name back. There was some pushback, but I was adamant about that. I'll help you say it, but you're going to call me Thresette. I want to be called by my first name because I always liked my first name. I was just making it easier for others when I went by Kay.

> That part of embracing who I am was awesome. Just using my

uniqueness. Because you won't find another person in this world named Thresette, except the lady I was named after who has unfortunately passed away. I think my authenticity about what I was experiencing and why—and then learning to embrace it—was truly a source of strength in my leadership. Here I am. This is who I am. This is me. I can't help it. And you have to accept that.

Authenticity is the quality of being genuine or real. When talking about a leader expressing authenticity, it refers to someone being themselves, not pretending to be someone or something they're not, and not pretending to be perfect when we all know that nobody is.

In an article in the *Harvard Business Review* titled "The Authenticity Paradox," author Herminia Ibarra states that an important part of growing as a leader is viewing authenticity not as an intrinsic state but as the ability to take elements you have learned from others' styles and behaviors and make them your own. She discusses a study of investment bankers and consultants who were promoted into new roles advising clients and selling new business. To gain confidence in their new positions, some of them consciously imitated styles and tactics of successful, established leaders, such as learning how to use humor to break the tension in meetings and how to persuade without being arrogant. Essentially, they tried different approaches until they found what worked for them. As a result, the imitators arrived much faster at an authentic but more skillful style than the others in the study, who focused solely on demonstrating technical mastery and had a harder time with imitation because it felt fake to them. Those individuals were perceived as unable to adapt and were less successful in the new positions.[11]

Mali Phonpadith, Founder of the SOAR Community in Alexandria, VA, told me,

I feel like the leaders who have mentored me to become a better version of myself have been willing to be vulnerable. They're wonderful storytellers. They're authentic about their trials and tribulations. They talk about their scars, what they suck at, and all the things that they've stumbled on and messed up in life. And then I try and remember how those mentors and leaders made me feel, how supported I felt, how seen I felt, how I didn't feel less than, or they were better than, or they weren't looking to be anybody's guru. They are human beings who are on the journey themselves, and they may be a few steps ahead of me or many, many years of experience ahead of me.

And that's the type of leader I have practiced being. Do I always get it right and know that I do my very best to be vulnerable even when it's uncomfortable for me? No. But I know that maybe the person that I'm leading or my strategic partners need to see the more vulnerable side of me so they can feel that trust level. When somebody else recognizes that you are stretching yourself, that you are peeling away your own onion or taking off the mask, they just feel okay. If they're willing to do this and put themselves out there, then they're really leaning into inviting me into a deeper place where it's not superficial. Where I want you to understand that this is hard for me, but the trust is more important. The ability for us to work together. The ability for us to communicate together is more important. So even though this is scary, I'm going to tell the truth. I'm going to tell you some things that I wouldn't put out there on social media. And I feel that with honest conversation. When someone is uncomfortable when someone is showing the reality of what's going on, it's not always pretty, but I often find it's very much appreciated.

While authenticity means being yourself, it doesn't mean you can be a jerk, even if that's your real personality. It also doesn't mean you should express every thought or fear that comes into your head. It's important to recognize the appropriate time and place for disclosing your weaknesses and/or struggles. Disclosing insecurities or uncertainty in a situation where your team needs strong leadership could cause severe damage to your reputation and lack of confidence in your leadership.

Jenni Romanek, Director of Analytics at Instagram, told me,

> One of the things I really pride myself on as a leader is being authentic and, to the extent possible, bringing my whole self to work. I think that has enabled me to build really strong relationships with my peers, with the leaders at Instagram, and also with my team because they know I'm being real with them, and they know what to expect, and there isn't a layer of interpretation around what I say trying to translate it into plain English. And it's really important to me to share with my team what's going on for me personally so they feel like it's okay for them to have personal lives too. It's okay for them to have times when there's things going on outside of the office. To acknowledge what's hard or distracting, and to normalize being a whole human and not just an automaton.

> So that's really important to me. And that also links to humility because I'm doing the same things with my free time that my team is doing. I like the same books and movies and restaurants, and we're the same humans. We're all made of the same stardust. And the thing that's awesome about that is it also means people feel comfortable coming to me when something's going wrong. And it feeds this virtuous cycle of I'm authentic and vulnerable, and that makes me more approachable, and then people do approach me when there's something going on.

So if there's something that's not right, I can really quickly help resolve it as opposed to having lingering major issues in the organization that I'm unaware of. I always say that if I don't know about a problem, I can't fix it. And the other piece of that is when someone brings me a problem, I do fix it, and I feel accountable for it. I follow up on solving the problem, but I also follow up with the person who brought it to me and make sure that they know what I've done, what's changing, what they should expect. And that again is part of this virtuous flywheel of building trust. It all comes back to that.

One reason people fear authenticity is because it means they must be vulnerable, and that can be scary. By exposing and communicating their struggles and failures, effective leaders demonstrate vulnerability. In her book *Daring Greatly*, Brené Brown defines vulnerability as "uncertainty, risk, and emotional exposure." She goes on to say that every act of courage requires vulnerability. When you think about acts of courage, can you identify a single one that doesn't require uncertainty, risk, and emotional exposure? I can't.

Showing your authentic self to people is an act of vulnerability and an act of courage. You're opening yourself up to rejection, to people thinking you're weird or not liking or trusting you. But without doing that, you'll never form the connections necessary to influence and lead people effectively.

Lisa Marie Platske, President of Upside Thinking and a leadership coach, told me that she used to struggle with authenticity. She told me about a time that she hired a marketing consultant who told her that her communications were sterile and had no personality:

She said, "It just needs more of you in it." I thought that's the stupidest thing; how can I be more of me? Ridiculous. You know, when people tell you to be yourself, it's like, who else do you think I was being? And that, for me, was annoying. And at the same time, it changed my writing and my upside thoughts where I began to disclose things more and more, disclosing things about me, the things that I didn't get right, as well as the things that I did well versus just sharing the pretty picture. And after that conversation with her, while I didn't necessarily dive in, I would consider it like wading at the kiddie side of the pool and then going, "Okay, I can do this." Now I can go under and wet my head. It was more like that. It wasn't an immediate dive in the deep end.

I discovered that there were pieces of me that I didn't want to look at. So the journey of authenticity for me in disclosing more of myself with others is that I learned more about myself, but I learned the very biggest lesson in leadership of all is that one of the highest leadership skills is forgiveness, both self-forgiveness and forgiveness of others.

Years ago, I would've been so ashamed of failing that I would never have shared my struggles. But now, I publicly share my failures and have really made friends with them because I forgive myself. That was a moment in time, and then I look for the lesson.

You know, I've gotten more clients because of it. My business has doubled. In fact, the type of clients I get now are seven- and eight-figure entrepreneurs and people who are corporate executives.

It brings up a lot of really interesting things that when you talk about vulnerability and being willing to put yourself out there and talk about your crap. Because people can feel you. You've gotta be in your heart, not in your head.

In a recent interview with *Women's Health* magazine, actor and Founder of The Honest Company, Jessica Alba talked about the importance of being authentic and vulnerable. She said,

> My husband's a vulnerable and open person, and his family are vulnerable and open and nonjudgmental. I think just watching them, and how they operate allowed me to feel like it's OK to be flawed, it's OK to feel, it's OK to mess up, it's OK to say sorry and keep it moving. It's a lifelong lesson.[12]

Kathy Wilson, a leadership coach and President of Coach Kathy Wilson in Alexandria, VA, talked about the importance of authenticity to connecting with others. She said,

> I feel as though not only do we, as women, not honor ourselves, I don't think we really know ourselves. I think we know who we take to work each day in order to survive. But what if you showed up as who you truly are and be fearless and showed that to others?
>
> As much as we'd like to think we can control outcomes, we actually don't have a lot of control over it. So we try to tailor our personality and who we are to avoid making bad things happen. I want to avoid people thinking that I'm weak, and I want to make people think I'm strong. I want to make them think I'm a good leader. It rarely turns out the way that we want it to. And we don't even recognize that that's sometimes the reason why we don't get promoted is because when we show up disingenuously. People don't say, "They're just afraid to be vulnerable or afraid to be authentic." What they think is, *Something's not right. They're hiding something. I don't know what it is, but it just doesn't feel right to me.*

We've all had that moment when we're around people in everyday life, and we're like, *I don't know if I can trust them*. I don't know why, but part of it has very little to do with whether or not they're trustworthy, as much as how they're showing up in that moment, which is not authentically.

This is going to sound so self-help-y, but I've done a lot of work not to carry shame around things from my past, like having been bullied or having been suicidal, about the color of my skin, and all of these things that I had shame around. I felt like I had to act like this because people are going to have these stereotype ideas. So I did a lot of work on just being like, yeah, all of that is part of this amazing quilt that is me. It is so unique, and you can't cut out the bad bits of the quilt, or it will never keep you warm.

So why not just settle in and love yourself and take the lessons from all of those things that you might feel shame around and applaud yourself for surviving and say, "Hey, that girl, look at her, she made it," and then take that into the world so that people can connect with who you truly are. And that's a tough ask, especially in organizations that are predominantly male. You have to be okay with your personal story.

Kathy continued,

I want to share another quick story about why I feel like this is important. I was raised with some pretty awful ideas around body image, and I was never heavy, but I was bulimic for a good portion of my school years, including while I was an athlete. So I took the coaching job at Ole Miss. And my first week on the job, the coach comes to me and says, "One of the girls can't practice. She hasn't been released for practice because she was bulimic, and they're afraid for her health. And I'm wondering if you'll talk to her."

I was just like, "Oh my God." So I've got two choices here. I can talk to her about her issues. Because she refused to go get help. She would not go see a psychologist. Or I can talk to her about me. And I had never shared my story with anyone. It was such a big source of shame for me. And I remember going home to my apartment that night. I was sick to my stomach. And the next day, I took her out for a walk, and I told her everything about my journey. And she just looked at me like, "You?" And I was like, "Yeah, so, you know, I am living proof that you can survive this." And she turned it around, was released to play; I think she was a sophomore at that time, and she played three years for me.

Then I got to GW and had three more girls in the same situation and shared my story. At that point, the story was less triggering for me, but it still wasn't easy. And now, years later, they're all better. One of them has three kids. Another one has two. I'm still in touch with them. You never know who you are going to inspire or help or help change by showing up in an authentic and vulnerable way that helps you to identify with the human side of other people.

If you want a position of leadership, but if there's no humanity in it and it's just about, "I want to be a leader, or I want the title, or I want to be able to lead people," then you're not seeing the humanity and the vulnerability and the gift in it. Then I think you're missing something so impactful. How do you teach other people to be leaders if you're not vulnerable and authentic? You have to teach them the skills, but also the humanity part of it.

CHAPTER TAKEAWAYS

→ Authenticity is the quality of being genuine, being real, being yourself, and not pretending to be perfect—a human being with both strengths and weaknesses.

→ People respond better to authentic leaders.

→ Fake authenticity will be recognized.

→ Being authentic requires vulnerability, which is uncertainty, risk, and emotional exposure.

Chapter 12

BE APPROACHABLE

BE ACCESSIBLE TO YOUR PEOPLE

"Engaging with the audience lets them know I'm approachable. I don't like that whole, 'You can't talk to Sheila E. thing'—I don't like that."

—SHEILA E.

When I became National Chair of NAWBO, I had a goal to make the board more approachable for our members. One of the complaints I had heard over the previous few years was about the perceived standoffishness of the board and their detachment from the chapter leaders and members. So I started a monthly event called ChairChat (a Facebook Live session in the private chapter leader FB group) to keep them updated on upcoming events and other happenings at the national level, answer questions, and chat about whatever concerns they had. I received a really positive response from the chapter leaders.

That fall, I went to our national conference feeling pretty good about how things were going. Our board was working well together, we had set some ambitious goals and were on track to achieve them, and the chapter leaders and members seemed really engaged in what we were doing nationally. Soon after I got there, I was walking through the hotel restaurant where the conference was being held, and a member stopped me as I passed her table. She said she wanted to thank me for the ChairChats. I told her I was very happy that she found them so valuable. She then explained that she regularly did FB Live talks for her business, and she always got really stressed out beforehand, worrying that she might stumble over her words or mess up in some way. But then she watched my ChairChats and realized that I messed up all the time, and that was okay, so it would also be okay if hers weren't perfect.

Approachability is about allowing yourself to be accessible to others, particularly those you are leading. Depending on the size and geography of your organization, that could mean popping into a new hire orientation to introduce yourself and say hello, having an open-door policy for people to come by and talk or ask questions, holding office hours when you're available for informal meetings, providing your email address to all of your employees and responding to their emails, or hosting a regular ChairChat on FB to interact. It could also mean being open to someone stopping you in a restaurant to let you know that your imperfections inspire them (see also, Chapter 13 on humility).

In the last chapter on authenticity, we discussed how you could be your true self versus projecting an idealized image. When we allow people into our bubbles, it makes connection possible. Approachability works similarly.

Approachability is key for effective leaders to demonstrate to connect with their people, instill loyalty, and increase engagement. Approachability puts people at ease and makes them perform at their best. If you are naturally shy or put up barriers to communication and make people think that you don't want them to approach you, you might not learn news or information you need to effectively lead your organization. Being in a leadership position automatically puts you in the driver's seat regarding communication; you have to initiate conversations and make yourself open to being approached before others will feel comfortable approaching you.

Lisa Rosenthal, CEO of Mayvin, a Defense contracting firm in Annandale, VA, agrees,

> You will never hear what is going wrong if you aren't accessible and approachable. Both right and wrong are equally important to hear. If you put people at ease, they perform their best. It is key to building trusting relationships with people you lead and with your leaders.

As previously discussed, to truly lead, your people need to feel connected to you. And they won't feel connected if you won't interact with them or if you act like you don't want to hear from them. According to a 2015 Gallup research report, open and approachable managers have more engaged employees. "Among employees who strongly agree that they can approach their manager with any type of question, 54 percent are engaged. When employees strongly disagree, only 2 percent are engaged, while 65 percent are actively disengaged."[13] Employee engagement has a huge impact on the success of every organization, so being approachable can mean the difference between achieving your goals and failing in the marketplace.

Jeanette Armbrust, Managing Director of Skyline Exhibits of

Greater Los Angeles, told me that she was complaining to her business coach about feeling like she was being interrupted all day long, even though she had told her employees that she had an open-door policy:

And my coach said to me, "Your whole job when you're at the office is to just be accessible to your team. The little things that you do, you can do them at home. You can do them after hours, but you should be grateful that they're knocking on the door to have a conversation with you because it shows that they feel able to talk to you. You feel approachable. They feel like they keep you plugged in. If you're somebody that has their door closed all the time, they'd never feel like they can talk to you. That is not a great way to run a business."

So it really changed my way of thinking; when I'm in the office, then my job at the office is to sit at my desk and get some stuff done, but if somebody comes in my office, stop and listen because that's where you get the real power in people feeling like you're connected.

And it gives them the ownership thinking and feeling like they have the ability to walk in and talk to the owner or the president or whatever. So I think for me, that's a game-changer as a leader that people feel comfortable talking to. I realized when I'm in the office, I'm there as the leader, and I sit at my desk, and I lead, and I'm leading people, I'm not leading processes. So now, I never shut my door unless I'm having a personal conversation that I don't want overheard. But my door is always open, and people can come in and talk to me.

And I also changed my approach, so in the mornings, when I

get to the office, I would go around to everybody's office and say, "Good morning, how are you today? What's going on?" And just that little gesture of reaching out to them made a huge difference. I mean, I had warehouse guys in the back that would hear the click, click, click of my heels on the concrete, and they would all freak out. And it was just for me to come up and say, "So Brent, how was your weekend?" And they'd be like, "Fine." But they never engaged with me any other time. So I would try to make a point to get back there regularly and just be a human to them and talk to them and thank them and tell them they're doing a great job.

So every Monday was what I called CEO day, and I worked at home because that was when I got my work done. I worked at home to get those projects done when I wasn't getting interrupted all the time. That was my thinking day. Get up at thirty-six-thousand feet, get that stuff done.

I think the leader has to take the initiative in that because people are afraid of the leader, especially if there are a lot of layers in your company. And a guy working in a warehouse making fifteen bucks an hour doesn't feel confident walking into the owner's office and starting a conversation or relationship. So the leaders have to take the initiative to reach out to everybody in the organization, not just the people who are their direct reports, to be approachable. But when you do, it really solidifies the team spirit. I think it just helps a company grow and builds on the team culture.

CHAPTER TAKEAWAYS

→ Approachability is about being accessible to those you lead so they feel comfortable talking to you.

→ Approachable leaders have employees who feel more engaged and appreciated.

→ Leaders who are approachable are more likely to learn about issues and problems in the organization.

Chapter 13

DISPLAY HUMILITY

DON'T PUT YOURSELF ON A PEDESTAL

"My mother helped me to be who I am: to have strength and not to let people run all over me and yet to be humble, to realize that all of this that I have today could be gone."

—MISSY ELLIOTT

As I was writing this chapter, Rachel Hollis, an author and self-help influencer, posted a video of herself responding to a follower who had commented that she wasn't relatable because she was bragging about having a housekeeper. In the video, she rants about how she doesn't want to be relatable, that she's so successful that people shouldn't be able to relate to her, and that she works harder than everyone else so she can afford the cleaning lady. She then compared herself to other "unrelatable AF" women like Harriet Tubman, Oprah Winfrey, Ruth Bader Ginsburg, Amelia Earhart, and Frida Kahlo.

The reaction to the video was unsurprisingly negative, so Hollis posted a non-apology saying that she wasn't actually comparing herself to those women and blamed her PR team. After the uproar, and after losing over one hundred thousand Instagram followers, she then posted another apology taking responsibility and acknowledging that the video and her initial response to the backlash were problematic.

There were many aspects of her posts that were problematic: comparing her accomplishments of writing a couple of bestselling self-help books and building a successful company with those of women like Harriet Tubman, who risked her life multiple times to free enslaved people, and Ruth Bader Ginsberg, who sat on the US Supreme Court for several decades and advanced gender equality in the United States; claiming that she deserved her success because she woke up at four in the morning and worked hard every day, which completely discounted the effort put in by millions of less-fortunate women (often women of color) who have to work two or three minimum-wage jobs to support their families; and referring to her housekeeper, very likely one of those who have to work multiple jobs just to survive, as "the lady who cleans my toilets" not once but twice.

Hollis hasn't been heard from, publicly, since the second apology post (as of this writing), but a lot of unflattering stories about her have appeared in the media since then. At a conference in 2019, attendees said Hollis gave a speech telling her followers, "I own you" because they would buy anything she endorsed. Former employees say that at her company leadership summit in early 2020, she told her staff, "I am so rich, I could just retire to Hawaii and never work a day again; that's how wealthy I am."

Some people think that being humble means having low self-esteem, feeling unworthy, or lacking confidence. I disagree with that definition. Humility is understanding that you are not more important than others but also not less important. Instead, it is an understanding that every human is equally valuable: a recognition that you are worth no more or less than anyone else.

I've heard it said that humility isn't thinking less about yourself; it's thinking about yourself less. The fact is that nobody who has accomplished something big got to where they are by themselves; they had parents, teachers, classmates, coaches, coworkers, teammates, managers, employees, spouses, friends, and many others who helped them succeed in one way or another.

People who forget that fact and credit only themselves for their achievements are generally not effective leaders. They are difficult to be around, they alienate others with their boasting, and often drive away those people who helped them in the first place.

The columnist Judith Martin, also known as Miss Manners, has been quoted as saying, "It is far more impressive when others discover your good qualities without your help."

Humble leaders can be confident. There's nothing wrong with being proud of yourself for a job well done. It's when you start thinking of yourself as better or more important than others that there's a problem.

Humility is often evident in leaders who have mastered some of the other leadership characteristics described in earlier chapters, such as servant leadership (Chapter 9) and authenticity (Chapter 11). These leaders shift attention away from themselves and focus on the contributions and needs of those around them. Humble leaders admit to their weaknesses, mistakes, and flaws. All leaders are human, which means nobody is perfect, and everyone makes mistakes once in a while. Humility lets others see you as a fellow human being.

Mali Phonpadith, Founder of the SOAR Community in Alexandria, VA, told me,

> What I've learned is that even though this is your organization, you want people to know that you're in it together. Being humble and not appearing as if you know it all is really important, even if it's your thing that you've launched. You have to allow others to shine, to give them the spotlight to show what they have to offer. Why have these beautiful leaders in your community who are looking for a platform who have so much content and smarts to share if you are going to take over the spotlight?

> So humility is about knowing when to step off the stage and let other people step on. I think that comes with the territory. Humility is also all those other things that we talked about: being vulnerable, being authentic, showing your scars and flaws and cracking jokes, showing how silly you can be. Being okay with telling people that you don't know what you don't know. And just being able to truly express who you are.

In an article in *Forbes* magazine, Jeff Hyman shared that a number of research studies have concluded that humble leaders listen more effectively, inspire greater teamwork, and focus everyone (including themselves) on organizational goals better than leaders who don't score high on humility. He cites a survey of 105 computer software and hardware firms published in the *Journal of Management* that revealed that humility in CEOs led to higher-performing leadership teams, increased collaboration and cooperation, and flexibility in developing strategies.[14]

There is a big difference between being confident and being egocentric; unfortunately, some leaders get so caught up in their own hype that they cross that line, like Rachel Hollis did. Lack of humility in a leader can be damaging to an organization. These leaders are focused on receiving glory and recognition for themselves, not focused on what's best for the organization as a whole. They think the rules don't apply to them and are more likely to act unethically and create toxic corporate cultures.

Lisa Rosenthal, CEO of Mayvin, a Defense contracting firm in Annandale, VA, sums up how all of these characteristics work together:

> Confidence is essential in being a leader, and you should be proud of your accomplishments. However, arrogance is not becoming or effective. I am personally a fan of the servant leadership model where the leader serves the employees, which requires humility and confidence without arrogance.

CHAPTER TAKEAWAYS

→ Humility is not having low self-esteem or low self-confidence; it is understanding that you are no better or worse than everybody else.

→ Leaders who lack humility are very difficult to follow because their focus is on themselves, not the organization and people they are leading.

→ Effective leaders are both confident and humble.

Conclusion

IT'S YOUR TURN TO STEP UP

"There are two powers in the world; one is the sword and the other is the pen. There is a third power stronger than both, that of women."

—MALALA YOUSAFZAI

We're at a unique time in the history of the world. Never before have so many women of all ages stepped up to lead in all aspects of society. Teenagers like Greta Thunberg, Emma Gonzalez, and Yara Shahidi are stepping up and advocating for the causes that are important to them. Young women like Malala, Rachel Cargle, and Jameela Jamil are stepping up and leading on issues like education, racism, and bullying. Many others are stepping up and building successful businesses. Countless women are climbing the corporate ladder and stepping into leadership roles in their companies, with ambitions to make it to the C-suite. Numerous others are running for office, taking on leadership roles in community organizations, volunteering in their kids' schools, and starting nonprofits. Now it's your turn to step up.

I hope this book has given you an understanding of the mindsets needed to be a more effective leader and how to connect both with yourself as a leader and with those you lead. As I stated in the Introduction, nobody has mastered every leadership mindset, and that's okay. The point is to identify those areas you need to improve in, then make an effort to do so.

Leadership is connection. Connection with yourself to get the voice in your head to become your biggest fan, banish imposter syndrome, develop confidence and resilience, demonstrate integrity, develop a growth mindset, and figure out how to not take things so personally. And connection with others by understanding that leadership is about serving those you lead and being empathetic, authentic, approachable, and humble.

To recognize where you currently are and identify where you can get better, rate yourself from one to five on each of the mindsets using the following scale:

1. I don't really understand this and/or I'm really bad at it
2. I definitely need to work on this
3. I think I'm okay at this
4. I do well at this most of the time
5. This is one of my strengths

MINDSET	DESCRIPTION	SCORE
Mental Chatter	Control the voice in your head; get it to support you instead of sabotage you	
Imposter Syndrome	Recognize that you are not a fraud waiting to be found out; you are just as qualified as everyone else	
Integrity	Lead in accordance with your values; always do the right thing	
Confidence	Be sure of yourself and your leadership; be comfortable in your own skin	
Decisiveness	Make decisions confidently and quickly; don't flip-flop	
Resilience	Don't let setbacks deter you; bounce back from failure	
Growth Mindset	Always be open to learning new things; understand that you can grow and improve over time	
Don't Take It Personally	Understand that it's not always about you; even if it is, let it go	
Servant Leadership	Leadership is about serving the organization and people you lead, not about serving yourself	
Empathy	Connect with people by putting yourself in their shoes & understanding where they come from	
Authenticity	Present yourself as who you really are; don't pretend to be perfect	
Approachability	Be open to connection with the people you lead	
Humility	Don't put yourself on a pedestal	
	Total Score	

Scoring:

- 13–26 You need to read the book again
- 27–39 You understand the concepts but need to work on the execution
- 40–53 You've got several attributes of a good leader and the potential to be great
- 54–62 You're a very effective leader
- 63–65 Go back and reread Chapters 11 and 13

How can you improve your score? Identify those areas where you rated yourself the lowest and focus on improving them. Reread the lessons learned from those chapters. Identify leaders in your community or in your industry who are strong in those areas and follow them on social media or reach out to them personally. It might also help to reassess annually to see where you've improved and which attributes you should focus on going forward.

See Appendix A for more information about the leaders quoted in this book and how to follow them. Read other books, watch TEDx talks, and listen to podcasts on these topics. Attend a SeaStar workshop through my company, the Vellamo Leadership Institute (www.vellamo-leadership.com), where we discuss how to apply these important leadership mindsets and skills in your life and career. Use code MYMREADER to get 10 percent off any program. I've also provided a list in Appendix B of some of the books I've read that will help you improve your leadership abilities.

My website, mollygimmel.com, also links to some of my favorite books, podcasts, and other resources to learn more about these leadership topics. You can also sign up for my newsletter.

You are already a leader. Now it's time to be the kind of leader that you want to be and that people are excited to follow.

ACKNOWLEDGMENTS

First and foremost, I want to thank all of the incredible women leaders who agreed to share their insights and stories for this book. Your willingness to be open and authentic made this book a valuable resource for the next generation of women leaders. I appreciate each one of you!

Second, I need to thank my wonderful parents, Carol and Jerry Gimmel, who have supported me all my life in all my various endeavors and who believed from day one that this book was worth writing and that I would do a good job of it. I don't know how I got so lucky to be your daughter, but I'm so thankful that I hit the parent jackpot. I love you very much!

Next, my business partner Diana Dibble and the rest of the D2DInc corporate team—Lora Adams, Diane Michie, Joyce Asiana, and Rick Whitson—thanks for holding down the fort and keeping the company going while I've been running around the country and the world for NAWBO for the past eight years.

Thanks to all of the fantastic Scribe Media folks I worked with—

publishing managers Erin Mellor and Becca Kadison, editor Nicole Jobe, cover designer Liz Driesbach, and everyone else on the Scribe team who helped get this book out into the world.

Thanks to my writing accountability partners Nika Kabiri and Sara Waters. If I hadn't had to check in with you every week and report my progress, I probably wouldn't have gotten the book done. I can't wait to read your books!

And finally, thanks to NAWBO and my NAWBO sisters in the Greater DC chapter and across the country. In the almost twenty years I've been a member, I've learned so much from you all about leadership, entrepreneurship, community, and so much more. I've met so many extraordinary women through this organization that I'm privileged and honored to call my friends and mentors. Thank you for all that you've given me.

Appendix A

MEET THE LEADERS

Ildi Arlette created Results Continuum Inc. in 1994 as a premier HR consulting and training company. Since 2004, Ildi has specialized in consulting for 350-plus leaders and teams in the medical aesthetics field to achieve their business and personal goals. Her focus is to increase business results by elevating levels of leadership, staff engagement, and client service. Ildi has a proven track record as a results-driven leader, industry expert, thought-leader, coach, and business partner. As a business leader for over twenty-five years, Ildi greatly values the hard work and dedication of clinic and business owners, service providers, and entrepreneurs. Learn more about her at resultscontinuum.com.

Jeanette Armbrust is originally from the Pasadena, CA, area. She attended UC Irvine and then started her career path in the entertainment industry for BMG/RCA Records before moving to Minnesota to work for VEE Corporation, the creators of Sesame Street Live. There she was the National Promotion Director coordinating the touring events throughout North America. Later she was promoted to National Sponsorship Director. Jeanette started Skyline Exhibits of Central Ohio in Columbus, Ohio, in

2001. After growing her company into an award-winning seven-million-dollar business, she sold the company and found herself back in California as the Regional Managing Director for Skyline. Jeanette is also a certified executive leadership coach through The Academies CELDC (Certified Executive Leadership Development Coach) program and a JoAnn Davidson Leadership Group graduate. Additionally, Jeanette is a past Chair of the NAWBO National Board of Directors. She was named one of the 2017 Enterprising Women of the Year and the SBA Small Businesswoman of the Year. She previously served on the board of NAWBO Columbus as President, the Columbus Chamber Board of Directors, and is a member of Executive Women International and WELD, and she is the Founder of the Columbus Young Entrepreneur's Academy.

Melanie Thomas Armstrong is the Founder and owner of Through-Line Consultants, where she uses genetic genealogy to generate investigative leads that help law enforcement close cold cases. She is a retired PricewaterhouseCoopers (PwC) partner and a senior executive with eighteen years of experience at the partner and C-suite level, seven of those as a Chief Operating Officer (COO). She has been a partner at four firms: PwC, Guidehouse, Unisys, and Arthur Andersen. She established and led PwC's (now Guidehouse's) US International Development practice focused on social impact work addressing critical challenges faced by underprivileged people around the world. She began her career as an auditor and spent two years working in the Czech Republic as it converted from communism to capitalism. She sits on the boards of two international NGOs: Mercy Corps and Leadership Mission International. She is also working on her first book about her time in the Czech Republic. Melanie holds a BA in psychology from the University of California, Los Angeles. She loves to travel from her home base in Virginia, where she resides with her two teenage children.

Darla Beggs is the President and CEO of Abba Staffing and Consulting, Abba Parking Services, and MGD Management Group. Her broad business experience includes consulting with HR, insurance, and oil and gas professionals to evaluate and establish effective programs focusing on cost-effectiveness coupled with employee satisfaction and retention. She has succeeded in balancing the needs of the employee population with cost-effective solutions for business clients to provide solutions that provide a "win-win" solution at every turn. In 2011, Darla was appointed to the National Board of Directors of the National Association of Women Business Owners (NAWBO), where she served on the Executive Committee and assumed the role of National Chair from July 2014–June 2015, and on the Executive Committee of the National Board of the NAWBO Institute for Entrepreneurial Development, where she served as National Board Chair from July 2015–June 2016.

Thresette Briggs is Founder and Chief Performance Officer of Performance 3 (P3), a certified, national woman and minority-owned leadership development firm headquartered in Indianapolis, Indiana with offices in Roanoke, Virginia. P3 believes every leader can be high performing with the right opportunity and the right culture, and helps leaders in small business and diverse, global companies achieve both through keynotes, training and facilitation, and coaching services delivered through conferences, leadership meetings, learning series, retreats and strategic planning, and workshops. An author and sought-after speaker, Thresette inspires leaders to create a mindset and voice for sustainable high performance. Her honors and recognition include local and national boards and committees, features on billboards, commercials, podcasts, and voice talent for Emmy and Telly Award-winning production companies. She received her BBA from Wichita State

University, her MBA from Indiana Wesleyan University, and owns two services registered with the United States Patent and Trademark Office. Follow Thresette on LinkedIn (linkedin.com/in/thresette/) and visit Performance 3 at bestperformance3.com.

Penny (Benkeser) Thompson owns nine Servpro franchises in North and South Carolina, in addition to Carolinas Restoration, a construction company. Before her entrepreneurship ventures, she worked in various leadership positions in Corporate America, including Bank of America and Ford Financial Services. She has served in leadership roles in the National Association of Women Business Owners (NAWBO) and is a member of Vistage in Charlotte, NC. You can connect with her on LinkedIn at linkedin.com/in/pennythompson.

Elizabeth Bennett-Parker is Vice Mayor of Alexandria, Virginia, and in 2021 was elected to the Virginia House of Delegates in the 45th District. As Vice Mayor, she serves as a member of the Alexandria City Council and is the youngest woman elected to Council in Alexandria's history. Born in Alexandria to two Naval officers, Elizabeth is dedicated to serving her community. She co-leads Together We Bake, a nonprofit job training and personal development program for underserved women. Elizabeth is also the Founder of Fruitcycle, a business fighting the tragic paradox that, while one in six Americans experience food insecurity on a daily basis, 40 percent of our food is thrown into landfills. Before launching Fruitcycle, Elizabeth worked for the National Governors Association, where she served as governors' liaison to Congress, federal agencies, and the White House on issues related to transportation, economic development, and health. Selected as one of Alexandria's 40 under 40 in 2017, she has served on the Community Criminal Justice Board and the Commission on Employment, as well as the boards of the Arcadia Center for Sustainable Food and Agriculture, Agenda: Alexandria, and the United Way Regional Council for Alexandria. She is a graduate of Emerge Virginia and the Alexandria City Academy. Elizabeth served as a Fulbright Fellow, graduated Phi Beta Kappa from Cornell University, and earned a master's from the University of London.

Jessica Billingsley is the Chief Executive Officer & Board Chair of Akerna, the most comprehensive technology ecosystem for cannabis operators, governments, and brands. She is an accomplished innovator, executive, and board member in public and private international technology with over twenty years of experience. She co-founded MJ Freeway in 2010, where she served as President until April 2018, and later as the CEO until MTech acquired MJ Freeway to form Akerna. Shortly after, as CEO, Jessica led Akerna to become the first cannabis technology company listed on Nasdaq. You can connect with her on LinkedIn (linkedin.com/in/jessica-billingsley) or follow her on Twitter (twitter.com/jessbillingsley).

Lynda Bishop is the Founder and CEO of Summit Alliance Solutions, an international coaching/training/program development firm. As a master's-level mental health therapist and certified empowerment and executive coach, Lynda has developed and facilitated groups across the United States and China for over sixteen years. She currently contracts with national women's leadership organizations and entrepreneurial support organizations in program creation, management, and impact expansion. As the Vice President of National Programs for the National Association of Women Business Owners, she spends her energy and talents doing what she loves most: supporting women leaders. You can find her on LinkedIn (linkedin.com/in/lyndabishop), Facebook (facebook.com/lyndakbishop), or Instagram (instagram.com/lyndakbishop).

Kristina Bouweiri is the CEO and President of Reston Limousine, Washington DC's premier transportation provider, ranked among the nation's top ten largest luxury transportation operators. Starting with only five vehicles in 1990, Bouweiri diversified the business and developed Reston Limousine. Today it is a thirty-million-dollar company with over 250 vehicles from sedans to coach buses. Kristina also is the Founder of the networking program Sterling Women and Co-founder of the Virginia Women's Business Conference, two programs that have helped hundreds of women entrepreneurs and executives achieve their professional goals. Follow her here: linkedin.com/in/kristinabouweiri, facebook.com/kristina.bouweiri, instagram.com/kristinabouweiri.

Dr. El Brown is the Founder of KinderJam and author of *Mama Bear: One Mom's Story of Optimism, Autism, Advocacy, and Love* and *Adventures of SuperDuperKid: Friendship Numbers*. She is also a faculty member at American University in Washington, DC. Early in her career, Dr. El served as an Elementary and Early Childhood educator in the United States, Japan, and South Korea. Upon her return to the US, Dr. El founded KinderJam, an Early Childhood Education care, enrichment, and training agency that has served young children and their families globally. Dr. El believes that families and service providers deserve exposure to high-quality skills and strategies needed to assist them in helping children maximize their potential. Therefore, her body of work represents her desire to help increase the capacity of families and help-giving professionals. Above all, she is the proud mother of a fifteen-year-old son on the autism spectrum, affectionately known as SuperDuperYoungMan (SDYM).

Tammy Dickerson is the Founder and CEO of TBG Events, a national full-service event production firm. Celebrated as a tenacious powerhouse, Tammy has partnered with Fortune 100 companies, politicians, celebrities, and global organizations to curate and produce over thirty national events annually with five hundred to over fifteen thousand guests. Tammy is a Founding Member of The Black Table, a collective group of Black event professionals in the entertainment and hospitality industry. She is also a proud member of Meeting Planners International Southern California Chapter (MPISCC) and the National Association of Women Business Owners (NAWBO). You can connect with her on LinkedIn (linkedin.com/in/tammy-dickerson) or follow her on Instagram (instagram.com/tbg_events).

Jen Earle has had the honor and delight of working with the National Association of Women Business Owners (NAWBO) since 2008. She currently serves as the CEO of NAWBO and the Executive Director of the NAWBO Institute. Utilizing her institutional knowledge and consistent drive to advance the mission of NAWBO, Jen works collaboratively with the National Boards of Directors to help carry out the Board's vision for the organization and navigate NAWBO to where it is today. Jen brings to the table more than a decade of multidisciplinary, high-level experience in operational and project management development, support, and execution for a broad range of boards, business groups, entrepreneurs, CEOs, and executives. She currently serves as an Advisory Board Member for *Enterprising Women Magazine*, Council member for the National Women's Business Council (NWBC), and Steering Committee Member for FCEM (World Association of Women Entrepreneurs).

Maria Gamb is the Founder and CEO of the training company NMS Communications. Considered a leadership expert, she dedicates herself to helping busy professionals create high-performance teams, make a positive impact, and maintain a balanced life. She has authored four books: *Healing the Corporate World, Values-Based Leadership for Dummies, The Resiliency Journal,* and *Gratitude Journal.* As a sought-after keynote speaker and thought leader, she has been featured in *Inc. Magazine,* in *Time,* on Wall Street Radio Network, and she has written for *ForbesWomen.* You can connect with her on LinkedIn (linkedin.com/in/mariagamb) or follow her on Instagram (instagram.com/maria_gamb).

Lisa Kaiser Hickey is the Founder and Chairman of the Board of DPRINT, an award-winning multi-technology graphic communications company in Orlando, FL. Ms. Hickey is a former President of both NAWBO and The International Alliance for Women (TIAW). She served Les Femmes Chefs d'Entreprises Mondiales (FCEM, an international association of entrepreneurs) as Regional Director for North America. She is a qualified Global Board-Ready Woman by the Forte Foundation and holds a Certificate in International Trade. She is a member and/or supporter of multiple global women groups, in addition to a certified John Maxwell leadership coach, trainer, and presenter—certified Everything DiSC and 5 Behaviors facilitator.

Monica Levinson is a prolific film and television producer with an expansive career, as reflected by the diverse array of projects she has produced. Working alongside top innovators in entertainment, she is frequently lauded for her passion to protect and further the creative aspects of filmmaking, with a strong commitment to fiscal responsibility. As a Women in Film board member and part of the leadership committee of the Women's Production Society, she devotes effort into gender parity and inclusion to be the norm. Recent projects include *Borat Subsequent Moviefilm, The Water Man, Wander Darkly, Captain Fantastic, Beirut, Brian Banks,* and *Trumbo.* Follow her on Twitter at twitter.com/monlev.

Olalah Njenga is the CEO of YellowWood Group, a consulting firm based in Raleigh, NC. An award-winning entrepreneur, an accomplished business strategist, and an advocate for the small business economy, Olalah partners with business leaders to transform ideas into objectives and objectives into outcomes. She worked in several enterprise operations, administration, legal, human resources, and technology roles before founding her firm in 2003. Olalah serves in national and state leadership roles and is a trusted media source for the BBC, NPR, the *New York Times*, Marketplace, Fox, and local broadcast affiliates. Connect with Olalah at linkedin.com/in/Olalah.

Jennifer Peek is the CEO of Peek Advisory Group in Kansas City, MO, providing strategic financial services for the mergers and acquisition process of small to mid-size companies, in addition to contract Controller and CFO services. She provides realistic leadership, strategic financial insights, and actionable advice developed from over twenty-five years of financial experience benefiting companies ranging from Fortune 50 to startups.

Mali Phonpadith is the Founder and CEO of SOAR Community Network (SCN), a certified Talent Optimization Leader, and Inclusive Behavioral Inventory certified consultant. She is a TEDx speaker, podcaster, and bestselling author. Her consulting firm, SCN, helps organizational leaders map their strategic priorities and then supports their growth by building C3 cultures where *Compassionate* leaders thrive, *Cohesive* teams drive results, and employees *Collaborate* and innovate. She is the Co-founder of SOAR Nebula, a global resource hub for transcendent leaders. Learn more about her firm at soarcommunitynetwork.com. Follow her on LinkedIn (linkedin.com/in/maliphonpadith) and Twitter (twitter.com/maliphonpadith).

Lisa Marie Platske is an award-winning leadership expert in human behavior. She has received accolades from the United States Small Business Administration and The International Alliance for Women and been recognized as one of the top one hundred women making a difference in the world. She left her federal law enforcement career after 9/11 to build Upside Thinking, Inc. (UpsideThinking.com). A member of the Forbes Coaches Council, she has trained or coached over one hundred thousand leaders around the globe. When she's not traveling, you'll find her in Kentucky wandering around the rolling hills of her farmhouse and retreat/event center. To connect with her, go to linkedin.com/in/lisamarieplatske.

Jenni Romanek currently serves as Director of Analytics at Instagram, where she leads a team of eighty-plus data scientists. Her team uses modeling, experimentation, and data analysis to identify the greatest opportunities and launch the best products and services to meet the needs of the over one billion people who use Instagram around the world every day. Prior to joining Instagram, Jenni led data science teams at Twitter and held roles in finance, economic consulting, and startups. Jenni is passionate about supporting individuals on their career journeys and is the Founder of the Women in Analytics Conference, an annual industry-wide event bringing together women data professionals in service of increasing networking, representation, and learning for the community.

Lisa Rosenthal is the CEO and Co-founder of Mayvin, Inc., a technical services-based contracting firm, and Level Up Ventures, an emerging angel investment organization. In less than a decade, her Team grew Mayvin from one million dollars in annual revenue to over seventy-five million dollars. She is an inspiring thought leader, entrepreneur, philanthropist, venture capitalist, and executive that brings a depth of strong leadership experience to the US Government and Industry, developed and proven over a twenty-five-year career.

Lesa Seibert is the Co-founder, CEO, and CFO of Mightily (mightily.com), an award-winning advertising agency named to the Inc. 5000 and Financial Times Fastest Growing Companies three times. Lesa joined the National Association of Women Business Owners (NAWBO.org) in 2007 and now serves on the National Board of Directors. Lesa serves on several other national, state, and local boards, as giving back to the community and supporting women business owners is very important to her. You can connect with her on LinkedIn (linkedin.com/in/lesaseibert).

Jennifer Urezzio is the Founder of Soul Language, teaching clients how to access their intuitive guidance to positively transform and expand every aspect of their lives. Jennifer is a master intuitive, author, teacher, and speaker. She founded her own business, Blooming Grove, Soul Language's parent company, in 2004 in response to her intuitive senses and ability to help others feel better about themselves both holistically and naturally, working closely with them to generate a feeling of strength and well-being. She specializes in helping people connect: to themselves, to each other, and to the Divine. She founded a new paradigm, Soul Language, which provides guidance for understanding our true nature and tools for accessing deeper levels of awareness. This new insight into how the Soul expresses itself is being embraced by top healers, lifestyle coaches, and CEOs all over the world as a method for helping people recognize their purpose and live from a place of power and truth. To connect with her, visit soullanguage.us.

Lauren Weiner, PhD, is the CEO and Co-founder of WWC Global, the largest federal contracting firm in Tampa, FL. The company's clients include the US Departments of Defense and State, the US Agency for International Development, and others. Over 70 percent of the staff is a military spouse or a veteran. Previously, Lauren worked at the Office of Management and Budget (OMB) in the Executive Office of the President. Her academic accomplishments include a bachelor's degree from the University of Michigan and a PhD from Dartmouth College. Lauren co-founded two nonprofit organizations: In Gear Career, now the US Chamber of Commerce Foundation's Hiring our Heroes Military Spouse Professional Network, and Homefront Rising, a bipartisan organization that educates military spouses for roles in politics, policy, and advocacy (wwcglobal.com).

Kathy Wilson, a former collegiate and professional basketball player and coach, is a speaker, Transformation Coach, and Principal of Coach Kathy Wilson, a leadership consulting and coaching company. Balancing the lessons she learned on the court with her knowledge in the areas of change, leadership, and organizational management, Kathy brings a unique perspective on how to challenge and shift mindsets, align behavior with goals and strategy, and help people take their personal and professional lives to the next level. For over fifteen years, Kathy worked with clients ranging from government agencies to higher learning institutions to Fortune 100 and 500 companies, as well as with a variety of organizations, speaking, coaching, and delivering training and development solutions that have empowered individuals to transform the way they work and live. Kathy currently works solely with women over forty looking to reinvent themselves, achieve their biggest goals, and create the next level of their lives in her "Your Next-Level Life" coaching program. She also hosts a weekly podcast called *For Kick-Ass Women Only*.

Appendix B

OTHER READING MATERIAL

If you're interested in taking a deep dive into some of the topics addressed in this book, here are other resources for your reading enjoyment:

- *Chatter* by Ethan Cross
- *The Secret Thoughts of Successful Women* by Valerie Young, EdD
- *Decisive* by Chip Heath and Dan Heath
- *Daring Greatly* by Brené Brown
- *Mindset* by Carol Dweck
- *Grit* by Angela Duckworth
- *Think Again* by Adam Grant
- *The Confidence Code* by Katty Kay and Claire Shipman
- *The Leadership Gap* by Lolly Daskal
- *Dare to Lead* by Brené Brown
- *The Hard Thing About Hard Things* by Ben Horowitz
- *Values-Based Leadership for Dummies* by Maria Gamb
- *The High 5 Habit* by Mel Robbins

ABOUT THE AUTHOR

MOLLY GIMMEL is the Co-founder and CEO of Design To Delivery Inc, a four-time Inc. 5000 award-winning government contracting firm. Shortly after starting D2DInc, Gimmel joined the National Association of Women Business Owners (NAWBO), where she has served in a variety of leadership positions in both her local chapter and at the national level.

She also serves on the advisory board for *Enterprising Women* magazine and as a delegate for the United States on the W20—the working group of the G20 that focuses on women's issues. In 2021, she founded the Vellamo Leadership Institute to help women be more effective leaders.

NOTES

1   Jack Zenger and Joseph Folkman, "Research: Women Score Higher Than Men in Most Leadership Skills," *Harvard Business Review*, June 25, 2019, https://hbr.org/2019/06/research-women-score-higher-than-men-in-most-leadership-skills.

2   Allyson Bear and Roselle Agner, "Why More Countries Need Female Leaders," *U.S. News & World Report*, March 8, 2021, https://www.usnews.com/news/best-countries/articles/2021-03-08/why-countries-with-female-leaders-have-responded-well-to-the-pandemic.

3   Zing Tsjeng, "Lizzo: 'I'm Not Trying to Sell You Me. I'm Trying to Sell You, You,'" *British Vogue*, November 9, 2019, https://www.vogue.co.uk/news/article/lizzo-british-vogue-interview.

4   Pauline R. Clance and Suzanne A. Imes, "The Impostor Phenomenon in High Achieving Women: Dynamics and Therapeutic Intervention," *Psychotherapy: Theory, Research and Practice* 15, no. 3 (1978): 241–247, https://mpowir.org/wp-content/uploads/2010/02/Download-IP-in-High-Achieving-Women.pdf

5   Jeanne Croteau, "Imposter Syndrome—Why It's Harder Today Than Ever," *Forbes*, April 4, 2019, https://www.forbes.com/sites/jeannecroteau/2019/04/04/imposter-syndrome-why-its-harder-today-than-ever/?sh=745c3d659ac5.

6   Tavi Gevinson, "I Want to Be Worth It: An Interview with Emma Watson," *Rookie*, May 27, 2015, https://www.rookiemag.com/2013/05/emma-watson-interview/.

7   "The Cast of *Girls* Looks Back on Six Years of Friendship and Fights in the Ultimate Exit Interview," *Glamour*, January 3, 2017, https://www.glamour.com/story/the-cast-of-girls-glamour-february-cover-interview.

8   Ruchika Tulshyan and Jodi-Ann Burey, "Stop Telling Women They Have Imposter Syndrome," *Harvard Business Review*, February 11, 2021, https://hbr.org/2021/02/stop-telling-women-they-have-imposter-syndrome.

9   Risa Gelles-Watnick and Andrew Perrin, "Who Doesn't Read in America?" Pew Research Center, September 21, 2021, https://www.pewresearch.org/fact-tank/2019/09/26/who-doesnt-read-books-in-america/.

10 DiSC is a personality assessment that organizations use to help people better understand their coworkers so they can work together more effectively. People are scored on four personality elements Dominance, Influence, Steadiness, and Conscientiousness. Learn more at www.discprofile.com.

11 Herminia Ibarra, "The Authenticity Paradox," *Harvard Business Review*, January–February 2015, https://hbr.org/2015/01/the-authenticity-paradox.

12 WH Staff, "Jessica Alba on Big Business, Burnout and Being Vulnerable," *Women's Health*, August 5, 2019, https://www.womenshealth.com.au/jessica-alba-womens-health-cover-september-2019/.

13 Jim Harter and Amy Adkins, "Employees Want a Lot More from Their Managers," Gallup, April 8, 2015, https://www.gallup.com/workplace/236570/employees-lot-managers.aspx.

14 Jeff Hyman, "Why Humble Leaders Make the Best Leaders," *Forbes*, October 31, 2018, https://www.forbes.com/sites/jeffhyman/2018/10/31/humility/?sh=1760125c1c80.